How to
Live Free
in a
Dangerous
World

SHAYLA LAWSON

Tiny Reparations Books

How to Live Free in a Dangerous World

A DECOLONIAL MEMOIR

An imprint of Penguin Random House LLC
penguinrandomhouse.com

LIBRARY OF CONGRESS CATALOGING-IN-PUBLICATION DATA
has been applied for.

ISBN 9780593472583 (hardcover)
ISBN 9780593472590 (ebook)

Printed in the United States of America
1st Printing

BOOK DESIGN BY KATY RIEGEL

This book is a work of memoir. Some names and identifying
details of certain people mentioned have been changed.

For Phoebe

Revisiting this text almost fifty years after I wrote

it, I might call it something like "memoirs of a life

dedicated to the quest for freedom."

—*Angela Davis: An Autobiography*

Contents

[xi]

Contents

How to
Live Free
in a
Dangerous
World

Our story starts in an airplane with the sound of long acrylic nails tapping on laptop keys, the sound of black femme poetics . . .

On Firsts

Minneapolis, Minnesota

Let's begin at the beginning.

The weather is winter. The time, 1981. The only place in the world to be, Minneapolis. First Avenue & 7th. A music venue. First row. The artist is local—years from now, everybody who wants to be anybody will lie and say they had tickets, but you do. Three. Half-smiling on the dashboard of a Chrysler station wagon. One hundred miles south, in a blizzard, back tires sunk in eight feet of snow.

Most of what follows is meant to be true and what's not, probably even more so. Outside the car, the muffled buzz of "Soft and Wet" rocks the wood-paneled LeBaron, the bass replaced by the car engine, exhaust coughing holes through chunks of ice. Two men huff and slip in matching pairs of wing tips while their shovels scratch out a hard timpani on the gravel. Polished, ruined. Inside, the car is dark and hot, the windows blind with fog. The woman in the back seat opens her coat as pearls of sweat unzip down her chest. She scoots to the console, turns the defroster on high, and switches the cassette in the tape deck. *Dirty Mind.* The windows start to clear. She wipes a spot clean on the windshield with the back of her dress sleeve, gold lamé, and its streaks make the streetlamp under snowflakes look like a strobe light. The vents scream loud and crowded over the song on cassette and she lies back on the crushed velvet interior, tapping her pregnant belly. Everyone will say that they made it, but you were actually there.

My parents. I'm there too. Barely alive, just a thrum under the heartbeat of the woman who knows all the words to "When You Were Mine" in the front row. Prince was first and I was second. This became my origin story. Of the two men we came with, it took me a while to know who was actually first, my father, the three of them so thick as thieves by the time I was born it was more conceivable that I was the child of all three of them than one or the other. This was their gift to me. A black and brilliant world. A world full of music that knows the cold. A promiscuity that understands destruction. A few years later, one of the men left us all behind to become an astronaut, the first Black man to walk in space. And so began my family.

In the beginning was darkness and Prince was music. Everything I remember about the womb carries the sound of arpeggiators. When I came out, it took me longer than most to understand I do things differently. I wasn't built for anything but. I wanted to be Prince-like. And so I was. A star floating above the stage like a blade of tinsel. An actual star. Fiery, and patient, hurtling through the sky. By the time "When Doves Cry" became a hit single, I was two years old, and the story'd been threaded through so much of my youth that I remembered it like it was my own memory. And hopped around on unsteady legs singing *Maybe I'm just like* . . . in a ruffled dress like I understood those words. To be earthly is still alien to me. That I should be so terribly lucky.

At the close of a second encore, there I was: hugged by my mother, between my fathers, God and otherwise. I listened to the crowd's rumbling applause of *We love you, we love you,* unaware they adored anyone but me. If I had to choose, I couldn't have picked a happier beginning. My opening act taught me something. The road ahead is dangerous. You never know what's in front of you. But that shouldn't stop you from keeping the beat funky and showing up well-dressed. And just when you think you can take no more, life brings you, at least, one beautiful encore. What's come first is foreshadowing. How we begin is a metaphor.

I remember the first time I told a story. I still had baby teeth. But the memory plays like a song on muffled wood-paneled speakers—I can't make out the words but I still pick up the melody. Their laughter rippling on my heart like a drop of water. *We love you, we love you.* When there are so many wonders in the world, how do you recover?

I try not to.

Not every new thing's a beginning. I don't remember a single first day of school but I remember nearly all of third grade, where I learned to play chess and memorized an old Abbott and Costello routine, "Who's on first, what's on second," and "I-don't-give-a-damn" past third. Some firsts are so deeply imprinted, they're eternal. The skit's wisdom is as alive to me now as it was back then. First isn't about "who." It's what came next. Where we're headed after is anybody's guess. But since we're counting what got us here, we might as well begin at the beginning . . .

My first isn't the only start for which Prince is responsible. I think about Lizzo, first of her name, whose music Prince cosigned soon after the rising star arrived in Minneapolis. Her first big break? His song "Boytrouble." The feature validated her, made her, moved her. That's why firsts thrill me so much. It's where we lock legacies with each other. Being first isn't just about who you are, it's about what we become together. First. Who we become to one another. Second. All that's left is the choice to love. I don't give a damn who you are, we are the people. Electric, glittering, and about to burn out.

We need each other. That's the first survival rule of traveling. And we have a long way to go before we stop surviving and actually recover *from* surviving. But we can do that. We feed each other. Nowadays, I'm never homesick for the journeys I've taken, I'm hungry for the stories I know that bring everyone along; this firms us up for the long journey. There's no finish line. Just living. In concert, all of us rubbing bodies, whether we want to dance or not. We move, so we might as well be bumping the same decolonize mixtape. First thing to know: Minneapolis is a city that knows what good music sounds like. When traveling, you need those.

Minneapolis is Minnesota's only city. Calling St. Paul a "twin" is giving the town the same compliment you'd give a pretty girl with a smoke-show mom, just to be polite. Because it doesn't matter who's first but it does pay to be original. It's hard to be original. To be the first to believe in the beat in your mind and ask, *Will anyone else love my music?* It's imagining and seeing beyond. *Will anyone else love me?* You know it won't last—like sex, like snow—but we all love a good beginning. You know that song by Foreigner, "Feels Like the First Time"? I don't. No matter how many times I play the rest I can only remember the chorus. Because that's all we need, the feeling so wet and ephemeral.

———

Let's cut to the scene where the thrall in the concert hall matches the square drumming nails of a young Bermudian working at an airport booth. The year is 2008. The weather is never winter. The musician is Yesha.[1] Nearly out and about, and "making far too much money for a twenty-one-year-old" at her day shifts in immigration. We meet for the first time, after the pandemic, and our stories intertwine like we've known each other forever. Here I am, in Bermuda meeting a Black woman who knows what snow is like. Knows how the world started. Our meeting breaks some new dimension. This brings me nostalgia; I get started all over again.

"Why did you move to Minnesota?" I ask her as I've asked my parents, imagining Minneapolis' cold chill on her skin while, in St. George's, our cold drinks sweat profusely. Her first answer is simple: she was supposed to attend music college. Her second answer is profound: revolution.

"Change," she says. While my parents dreamed of becoming heroes, so did she. The art, the artist, a commonality. And more. Lizzo arrived in 2011, after the passing of her father, and Yesha, after losing her mother—January 1, 2010. Yesha's band, the Mad Way Out, made way for Lizzo's, so to speak. The group was composed of Yesha, her best friend Madeline,

---

1   Ai-ee-sha, three syllables, like Another Bad Creation's.

and Mad's boyfriend Tao ("the Way"). Lizzo's first Minneapolis band was also a trio: the Chalice—Lizzo fronting a band,
alongside DJ Sophia Eris and singer Claire de Lune. It was
fate that all their destinies overlapped. It was inevitable Yesha
and Liz's "firsts" would be mistaken for each other's.

"I love your music," people would say. Yesha got mistaken
for Lizzo around town, never sure if the compliment was paid
in reverse, but sure it was a compliment meant to be paid forward. They weren't at odds, they were living the same dream.
That's the only way we make it out some truly terrible shit, is
by making the place we live beautiful. Making something out
of it. Maybe music, if that's how you're talented.

"We were on a couple bills together," Yesha says. "Liz and
I were both curvy and animated. The actual content of our
music was very different." Two big-boned Black women who
could spit, write, and sing,[2] clearing the roof off concert halls
covered in twelve feet of snow. Raising the roof into darkness.
Because they'd survived the worst and weren't afraid of what
happened if their music tore the hood off First Avenue. They
knew they were loved into being alive. Whatever came first
for them, they saw this.

"Minnesota is a place for beginnings," Yesha says, "a place
where a tiny seed can sprout into a rock star." In 2013, both
Yesha and Lizzo debuted new two-woman bands at South by

---

2   Shout-out to the other quadruple threats: Missy Elliott, Tarriona "Tank" Ball,
Leikeli47, Queen Latifah . . .

Southwest. Sophia and Liz, now a duo. Mad and Yesh going by DONNA. By that time, Yesha described her relationship with Lizzo as "colleagues working in the same building on different floors." Lizzo might have forgotten Yesha's name but always cheered her on when they saw each other. "D-O-N-N-A all caps, period!" Lizzo greeted the girls as they passed backstage. Always that way, a nod to the Minneapolis music dynasty. In a few more years, Lizzo would be a household name. But it was DONNA she dapped in the audience that day—first row, cheering her on—bumping fists with a "Hey, sis, what's up?"

That's why firsts are important. You don't have to be there to benefit from their beauty. You already are. Hello there. At some point, we have all been radicals in the wild regard of pulling ourselves up from the root, making sure we get enough water. It doesn't matter how you began. You did. And now we're here together. So what will we do but revolt, because that's all there is in front of us—change. Each turn around the Earth: a revolution. Aren't we terribly lucky to be alive? Hasn't it been nothing but heartbreak ever since?

Every time I believe I'm ending, I travel somewhere. Even in my "dirty," messy mind. I used to say taking a trip was just a coping mechanism. I know better now; it's my way of mapping the Earth, so I know there's something to come back to. So that I know we're still here. It's my way of reintroducing myself. Of saying, I am so very happy to meet you. I am so very pleased to meet—you are so welcome, I feel so very welcomed by you. I turn the engine on. I shovel my dreams out the blizzard. And you know, if I stick in there, there will eventually be music. I know that. I believe that you'll play it for me.

That's what I love about "lover" when Prince says it. He means it. Like, when we really live, being and being in love are the same thing. I love you enough to interrogate myself. To do everything I can to get you started.

●

How do you know when you've begun? When you have somewhere to come back to. The year is 2015. I take a plane to Minneapolis for the first time in thirty years. I'm in the midst of my first divorce. I roll the loss around my mind until it's purple and hoary. Candy hard. I meet a bald-headed man in a suit who offers to stow away my suitcase and I think, *It's not baggage we carry but the propensity to start over.* He is playing chess.

"You should castle your king," I tell him. The suit is uncertain that "castling" is a good move. And he should be. He's wearing a wedding ring. I was looking for a reason for him to slide over and distract me from my heartbreak. But I don't look up. I'm using my iPhone camera to apply matte lilac lipstick, Nars' "Pussy Control."

"Because when we land, I am going to Prince-party," I tell

him. I leave out the article. I'm headed to First Avenue. A Prince tribute. Some of the people I love most in the world are meeting me there. It feels like the first time all over again, like before I was born. The castle is the wrong move. The computer puts him in check. As we exit the airplane, the suit tells me, "Send me a pic when you're out on the First Avenue dance floor." I agree to oblige. One story ends, another finds itself, somehow.

When I arrive at First the sky is raspberry. It's March, just as it was when my parents arrived, but the weather is warm and I take off my coat before hopping out the taxi in my party clothes. I march right up to the door with my coat and my rolling suitcase. I throw down the mélange at coat check, the way I imagine my family did. We are lovers in what we share in common—the daring, the drama, the uncertainty—a humble hunger for this dangerous life. Before the show begins, I ask someone to snap a photo of me, blurry and hot pink. My lips pressed tight, I hear the opening bars to "Kiss," and I kiss, I kiss, I kiss you first.

On Blackness

Farai is drinking Zambezi lager behind the wheel of an evergreen Acura at three o'clock in the morning. I've been in Harare less than a couple of hours. The sky is pitch, anticipating the day as a vision of itself rising up again. Meaning: somewhere over on the glint of the horizon there's the gold-pink seam of a new day breaking upon New Dispensation, a new political regime and the end of Mugabe's thirty-seven-year reign, which began just a few weeks before I arrived in Harare. But tonight, in the sticky bucket seats, with the windows rolled down, our driver is drunk and the four of us are looking for a place that's still open to dance.

Farai, the driver, I've just met for the first time, but he's the friend of the Zimbabwean PhD student I followed back to her home during winter break. I finished graduate school two years ago but we always vowed one day we'd go back together. Or maybe she dreamed, and I promised; that's how I ended up traveling around the world: I hear *What if*, I say, *Let's go*. In my mind, I've already done it. In my mind, I've already conquered the heat of Harare before we've even planned the trip.

There was something about that first drive in the dark in a new place that felt fresh, despite the peril. At home, it was December 2017, the first year of the Trump era, and I felt liberated to have someone reckless in charge of my fate instead of the careful way I'd grown accustomed to living in the United States. I did my taxes. I buckled my seat belt. Everywhere I walked in America, I strapped myself carefully in. It was nearly January, the tension in my liberal home city hitting its dark edges, like the stiff crunch of crisp dead leaves.

I'd spent the better part of Trump's presidential pursuits covering his rise to power for *This Is Africa*, a South African news journal. The pay was confusing, it involved an elaborate bank transfer that whittled the funds down to about $50 per article, but stretching my hand across the Atlantic connected me to a broader world at a time when America itself was under siege. News cycle running us dead on an engine of fear. An engine that wouldn't stop because it was built upon the same principle as America itself: *You must kill whatever kept you alive because we are dying.* Always forgetting that if *we* do not, we do not. South Africa had already been there with its own dictator—and the ensuing fight to end the apartheid we still are facing. Blue versus red, the real race battle.

This Is Africa was a journal rooted in intellectual discourse and debates around a future. *The* future. Qualities I admired not only in the journal but in my editor, Percy Zvomuya, a Zimbabwean. I felt empowered working for them, recognizing that I was part of a global union who had always fought the oppression of those threatened by progress, a global majority. The phrase "This is Africa" was welcome invitation into survival. "This is America" was a phrase I only heard bolstering the bonfire of how backward we'd become.

And "This is American" is something I'm unable to say. I am American, but America loves to forget that. African Americans are still fighting for the right of full citizenship in the US, with our lives hanging in the balance. But I love America, because the Black experience is a very American experience. Music, dance, sports, fashion—our country's greatest cultural exports came from its African roots. Being a Black American can be real cultural capital when traveling, because the world sees us with more appreciation than our own country does. We are the image of pride worth imitating. I think of this story my mom and her Ghanaian friend used to tell about their eighties friendship. About the parallels of their teen years in the seventies on opposite continents. According to their conversations, West Africans started wearing Afros because the boldness of its style and its politics were a chic thing to be in line with. The rising promise of Black Power, a new order. But my mom and her friends all sported their Afros for one reason, as a way to reconnect with their African heritage, as a sign of solidarity.

It's why I like "Black" instead of "African American." "African American" references what divided us, continents, imagined delineations. "Black" represents what unites us, ideas. Watching hip-hop music videos in the Netherlands, I was surprised that Dutch, French, and South African rappers referred to Malcolm X and Dr. King when discussing freedom. I didn't feel safe in America, let alone free. What I got as an answer was that there was an international understanding that "This is Black culture" is defined by the stories of African American triumphs. I asked why European and Afrikaans freedom fighters didn't get shout-outs in the songs I knew.

"America is who we look to," an Eritrean-Dutch friend told me, "it's what people know." I understood what she meant, but I hadn't thought about it. Black America has worked hard to make sure we're heard. We are loud enough, audacious enough, to make sure the whole world knows it. But when the world prioritizes our images of freedom above all others, the big "B" in Blackness becomes America's way of marginalizing everyone else.

———

Loud isn't always the solution that's needed. I still want to know who is accountable for the freedom of Blackness in other languages. The poet Nikki Giovanni once said English is a terrible language because we "speak it, instead of speaking through it." Blackness can be like this. The need for capital-B "Blackness" as an ethnic modifier arose from slavery, not skin color. With the creation of an African diaspora came a need to find a unifying element. Since we are not all joined together by religion or skin color, culture became the substitution. But when we center that culture around American culture, we miss so much. Capital-B Blackness, despite its global appeal, is not a global unifier. It's one part of the Pan-African vocabulary, maybe the most popular but not the only one. The difference between [capital-B] "Blackness" and [lowercase] "blackness" is the difference between a shout and a whisper. Knowing the difference is a crucial travel skill. I like to think of Blackness as a lighthouse on the edge of an ocean. Blackness might lead the way, but it is blackness that fills the shores.

•

In Harare, the sky is pitch, lined with a pink-gold seam of dispensation stirring in the background, the car gliding over the crunch of crisp dead leaves. Farai, our night's guide, an up-and-coming contemporary novelist, is opening another beer. Some of the foam sloshes against the dashboard. I'm sitting in the back cross-legged, horrified, holding on to the door handle and my seat belt for dear life. Everyone else in the car is Zimbabwean. I look around in the dark and they're all quite calm, the bumpy fast-paced ride nothing for them. Farai looks at me. I believe he caught the whites of my eyes widening in the back seat as we hit a large divot and he launches into a monologue meant to soothe the car's only American.

"We're used to this," he says, "the freedom. The reason why you are having such a hard time adjusting to driving this fast on an empty road on this night is because you still think of yourself as Black. Because you're still expecting repercussions for your Blackness. Here there are no white police. Worst-case scenario, we get stopped by a cop who knows one friend of ours or another, we pay a fine, we move on."

Farai's words were direct, horrifying, and truthful. Blackness in America was rarely something from which I could "move on." But I didn't get a chance to respond because we'd arrived at a dance spot that still had the lights on and Afrobeats rattling the windows. He pulled the parking brake, self-satisfied, and hopped out of the car—my brain still banging against the engine behind him.

He was right. I hadn't been scared for my life because the

car ride was dangerous, I was scared of the car ride and my Blackness. I had never just been me. A Black man driving and dancing in a car full of us in the dark was a death sentence in America. I knew it. I was used to living in the margins, not in a country, and I had succumbed to the likelihood of my death by the most ordinary but unnecessary means.

I don't agree with fighting for the monolithic use of "Blackness" to describe all people of African descent. It's not enough. We need more language so that we "speak" to each other and not just through each other—through Dr. King, and Malcolm X, and the assumption that Blackness can represent everybody with African ancestry. As long as we do this, we limit ourselves. We say some of us are "in" and some of us are "out." In this age, we don't just need the summary version of the diasporic experience, we need every story. When we treat Black culture as the global ethnicity of the diaspora, we miss that there are black people everywhere who don't fit neatly inside it. I'm not just talking about expanding the vocabulary of Blackness for the sake of Americans and Caribbeans, I'm talking about thinking of people throughout the globe—Southeast Asia, the Pacific Islands, and the Middle East. In traveling to these places, I've had to be corrected because I assumed we were not the same, not part of the same origin story, but we are. If we let Blackness create division between "us" and "them," colonization wins.

———

On another night in Harare, I was drinking Manhattans with the son of a well-respected politician—the ex-boyfriend of my friend the PhD student—and his sister, an author. I had told them I too was a writer. In his newly purchased mansion, we were enjoying our drinks, hanging our feet over the empty pool. I told him I travel because I'm always looking for a story. He adjusted his spectacles.

"I can give you something to write about."

He dialed a British dignitary's number and exchanged a few pleasantries before he had arranged an invitation to the dignitary's palace. We left, and arrived, immediately. The dignitary greeted us at the door wearing a smart white linen top and flowing sea-foam trousers. She wore a warm smile but everything about her was crisp, from the cut of her sun-bleached bob to the finish on her syllables. Her skin was a tart, tan orange—Trump colored—which made the contrast between her and the baby who would nestle against her chest a striking tableau when a servant brought the infant over. We settled into steep wicker chairs on the veranda overlooking a view of lush grass and a modest canopy of trees. I looked back at the house, where evening lights were starting to warm the windows, and where the rooms were so crowded with contemporary African paintings that I could smell the oil paint through the cool breeze.

I sat across from the dignitary. She poured us each a glass of sherry. Her adopted Zimbabwean daughter clawed at her pearls, a babyhood brazen, voraciously unconcerned for the modesty in her mother's clothes. I drank my sherry and tried to take a secret picture but the flashbulb burned bright, exposing my complete amusement. It made for a completely incoherent sentiment: I should've been embarrassed but instead I felt self-satisfied, sugary slow. It was the first time I'd been black, the observer of what's next, as opposed to Black, the defender against all wrong.

"She's a beautiful child, you know," I said, shaking some manners into the flashbulb incident.

"She is a beautiful child," the dignitary agreed, and sometime later, feeling like the two of us were comrades, she leaned toward me to say, "You know, now that we've already come for Zimbabwe's rich land resources, we're coming for its next natural resource . . ." She looked at her daughter, bobbing on her knee with one hand gripping her necklace. Nobody said anything.

Sometimes in this world, whiteness and blackness have to look each other in the eye for their cannibalistic truths. I think about the fact the slave trade began with negations like that, about how many people we could sell and still be people. We got our answer. Every one of us. Every single one of us.

Most of the world's futures are decided over glasses of wine behind closed doors. In that world, the people of Zimbabwe fought, and won, the full citizenship still denied us in America. I know this, but, *How dare she.* That's all I could think of. I was angry. But I was still drinking the wine paid for by those ideas, smiling as I turned over its crystal. I was still calmed by the listless sound of the lawn sprinklers wasting water across miles of untouched farmland, just so the British dignitary could hold her Zimbabwean baby over something pretty to look at. I was at one of the most civilized and intellectual dinners of my lifetime. In my own way, I had benefited from the distribution of resources that made the dignitary comfortable. And yet, no one on the veranda seemed as surprised by the resource value put upon Harare's children as I was because they had already done the tally of what freedom for the rich costs. I felt guilty. I tried to look at the PhD student, the politician's son, and his author sister, expecting some revelatory cues about what to say now, but they all looked patient. I expected someone to say something. But there was no Blackness: no sideways glare, no attempt at insurrection that I could determine. I thought I was among my enemies. Like that old mom adage, *All skin folk ain't kinfolk.* What I learned is, all skin folk are kinfolk, some of us just speak differently.

But that's when I had to acknowledge limitations in "Blackness" as a description for everyone. Blackness speaks loudly, announcing our presence to everyone else. But blackness speaks quietly, asking us to communicate more subtly with one another. As awful as the dignitary's words were, she did not represent the future of Zimbabwe. She was the past, making one last desperate attempt at reclaiming sovereignty. With New Dispensation, she planned to move back to Britain with her adopted child and purchased art. As a Black person, I felt the need to be vocal about her offensiveness. But when my friends did not, I started to see I was othering myself. We were already the majority: the dinner party, the maids, the adopted baby against one lonely, outmoded colonial power. This is "blackness." The ability to see us in spaces where we are not powerless. Where we have the choice to become not Black—not one definitive picture of greatness—but whatever we want.

I don't think of Blackness and blackness like the Marvel film *Black Panther*, my continent and the Continent wearing slightly different clothing while holding hands. I'm talking about something deeper: Americans recognizing that our desire to define Blackness as something to unite us actually commodifies us; it limits who we can be in America and beyond. As Americans, we apply our Africanness like an ill-fitting commodity. Our adoration of our "homeland" is understudied and indiscriminate—a mix of kente cloth, shea butter, cowrie shells, and descendance from kings, sold at urban heritage booths. I'm not saying this is bad. I'm just saying Blackness is American Africanness. We long to be reconnected and miss the ways we are severing those connections. We long to be connected and miss the ways we already are. We romanticize a Blackness that carries markers we can identify: where you fall in love with someone in a Flatbush Avenue dashiki, their first Black Power Afro pick, and an eight-millimeter film camera. Someone shy, curious, and carrying either Giovanni's *Black Judgement* or some specific academic text on Ifa. We African Americans are in a constant flirtation with our African discovery, but as America, we think we know everything, although it's obvious we're still trying to learn who we are.

Back in the car, everyone was drunk and cackling.

"Girl, when your camera lit up I nearly died," said my friend. I thought it was a joke, but then I heard it. We were on the dignitary's private land. Immune from any way my Blackness might have been a threat to her. And she opened her mouth to tell me the world's biggest, most unsecret secret. Sometimes, your people whisper to you: blackness. It's a language I want us all to learn. Being able to speak it is how Zimbabweans sharpen their skills of self-awareness; it's why their greatest resource is their intelligence.

•

In private, I'd never heard a group of young people speak more urgently about the affairs of their state. It was New Dispensation and it was summer. A heat was brewing in the land and in what they could become, and they argued about it, passionately, in bars where waiters shuffled back and forth with plates of spicy wings and cool bottles of Zambezi.

Young Zimbabwe had grown up with a president who was elected as a revolutionary and resigned as a dictator. There was so much for me to learn from them, heading into my years of Trump, but so much of it I couldn't absorb at the time. What stuck with me was adjusting to the frequency of change. Eighties babies and beyond, the young Zimbabweans I met watched their country shift from the British colony of Rhodesia into independent Zimbabwe with Mugabe as the catalyst for its socialist redistribution of wealth. It was a time of speed. The way they described it, a father could go to work one week as a high school math teacher and be elected as a finance cabinet member the next. Moving black people into positions of power after generations of colonial rule was swift justice, but it didn't come without the eventual price of violence. We can't make every dream we have to advance possible, I am learning. But what was beautiful about what Zimbabwe built from under Mugabe was a generation of young bourgeoisie who grew up reflecting pragmatically on the perils of an authoritarian government.

New Dispensation meant another chance. Their conversations each night were about how to be ready for it. What they would be called upon to do when the time came, and whether or not it was better to be abroad to make that impact. Most of them enjoyed a comfortable, bohemian upbringing, thanks to Mugabe's dictatorship, but as I'd seen in countless cities across the globe, local jobs were scarce for fiery intellectuals, and most of them would have to find their fortune elsewhere and bring that status back into the country, in whatever ways the future allowed.

I spent my last days in Harare running the streets as if I had been lucky enough to briefly feel adopted as one of its children. I met the Monkey Nuts, the city's indie rock band. Their style reminded me of back in the day when I first found Bad Brains and Living Colour—bands that weren't "Black" enough for the mainstream but black beyond measure—the faded scent of a selfhood that is proud, isn't meant to survive, but always makes it. The Monkey Nuts were the resident artists of the National Gallery of Zimbabwe, the city's main museum, the most popular hangout hotspot for local young creators. Of the cities I've visited, this was the first time a museum was a place of collection not just for the art but for the intelligentsia who lived there. The merger makes so much goddamn sense. Local pop stars driving power back to the creative people whose work lined every corner of the dignitary's living room, through curations of the avant-garde and after-hours rock concerts. A meeting place and an education. To be black in that world, in this time, what a treasure. We get to design the future. New Dispensation in its truest sense. That feeling many of us find in the rock shows of our youth, flinging around a dark basement, our feet trampling the flyers that brought us there into pulp beneath us. Or maybe just listening to the wind or reading a good book. Hell, be here. Zimbabwe taught me to be here because beauty always wins out. black is beautiful. Black is.

On Privilege

Roosteren, Netherlands

"What a pity you ended up here instead of someplace beautiful," says Marricka. We're driving on a highway through the countryside to which I moved a few months ago. Out the window the rain is soft and the grass is luminous. But what she means by "beautiful" is somewhere with more culture or more ease. Roosteren isn't a city, or even a town really. It's a village where, my Dutch husband and I joke to his relatives, "a 'traffic jam' usually involves a shepherd herding a flock of sheep across the road." With a long, curved staff and everything—it's biblical, really. Or what Condé Nast likes to call "idyllic." Like the provincial Netherlandish paintings Americans love to ogle at the Met.

I waded through a lot of early European and Renaissance art in architecture college. I prefer to look at art where everything is a mess, like the mixed mammal collages of Wangechi Mutu. But I'm adjusting to living every day like I'm in a Dutch landscape painting. I waddle along the internet on a cruiser bicycle wearing long skirts and braid pigtails into my hair.

At home, we live in a converted barn with a spiral staircase leading up to the bedroom loft. It's picturesque but also a pain in the side. I leave the spiderwebs in the high corners of the house to catch the mosquitoes because none of the windows have screens. My reason is simple but my logic lacks clear enough edges: when Kees' friends come over, they assume I'm a terrible housekeeper. They look at me pitifully, as if to say, "This won't last."

The first day I say that same thing to myself, a bird flies in our window. It's morning, we're newlyweds, we've just finished kissing and carousing, and in through the barn loft window flies a bird. At first, we talk it through as some kind of good fortune—a good omen—that a winged animal would take roost in the rafters of our little house. But as my husband jumps up to prepare himself for work, without ushering the bird out, I begin to feel that spiderwebs and a bird are far too much wildlife to explain away as welcome immigrants in our home.

"You'll figure it out," my husband says as he leaves, and I cower under the comforter with nothing but my eyes peeking out. I'm still naked. I'm scared the bird will shit on me if I make a run for my robe on the chair across the room.

But how? I think as he trots down the spiral stairs.

Kees moved from Maastricht to Roosteren before we got married, to be closer to his job at a pharmaceutical tech company. But time never seems to be friends with us. He's been fifteen minutes late nearly every day since I arrived—normal for me, an American now-housewife, but unforgivably late to Dutch working people. I wish he hadn't said "figure it out." I wish he'd stayed and helped me figure out the bird who was lost as I was. I cry for a while and, as soon as I get up, carry on with my day like the bird never happened. And the bird flew out.

My husband and I met while I was living in Harlem. Not Haarlem. He was on an extended layover in New York before flying to Brazil for a six-month backpacking trip through South America. My friends and I hosted a lot of backpackers through our international network of mutual friends and Gchat acquaintances. None of us had a ton of space but we each had a one-bedroom apartment with a pull-out sleeper sofa. Kees ended up spending a few nights with my close friend Paul, who lived across the street from me on 120th and Lenox. Kees' trip was just beginning but he'd lost all of his things—pulling an identical backpack to his from the airport carousel only to realize on the cab ride to his hostel that the backpack was someone else's, a woman's. He needed help, and so my little group of a dozen twenty-something Harlem do-gooders went to work organizing what supplies we could for him. For my part, I attempted to gather all of us together to take him out to dinner at a nearby pizza place. That night came but along for the ride was an icy, torrential late October rain. He and I were the only ones who made it. Our wedding invitations a few years later were postcards of us under the marquee to the pizza shop with a table for ten that only two of us ate at. It became our meet-cute, our first date.

Throughout the time that we dated he would come visit me in Harlem frequently. It's how I learned how much of New York, formerly Nieuw Amsterdam, still carried a Dutch imprint. Harlem (f.k.a. Haarlem) is a Dutch name. And so is Brooklyn, Long Island, Greenwich Village, and, of course, the Holland Tunnel. Even the word "Yankees," according to Kees' brother (whom Kees described as a "true Dutch chauvinist," the first and only time I'd ever heard that word used with love), was derived from an ethnic slur for Dutch people; it combined the names "Jan" and "Kees" and was used in the same way a New Englander might call his country cousin "Billy Bob."

Every time he introduced to me another new and foreign word, I would round it in my mouth, like a bite of an apple. I first heard "Roosteren" a few months before our wedding, as Kees emailed me pictures of the sweet, provincial renovation he'd just rented for us to move into, as I migrated from, essentially, one Dutch settlement to another. Likely caught by the prettiness of the house's staged golden-hour photographs and high loft ceilings, I assumed the word "Roosteren" meant "roost." I didn't know much more than a few Dutch words when I moved to the Netherlands. Aside from our conversations, I had been trying to learn from an illegally downloaded copy of Rosetta Stone. The first lessons helped me build one sentence—"De man is op on paard"—"The man is on a horse," which seemed like a completely useless first sentence to learn. Or so I thought, as that was before I ended up in a village, on a river, on the border of Belgium, that had a pasture where men with domesticated horses would sometimes ride alongside wild ones. The village was beautiful but boring, the way beautiful things often become—better in nostalgia than in the present. In New York, at home, when I didn't know what "Roosteren" meant and I made believe it was "roost," I was happy. Now that I lived there, and the bird and the bugs made it seem unlikely that I would be able to nest there, I began to understand I had naïvely deceived myself.

"There's nothing in Roosteren," Marricka went on, "it doesn't even mean anything in English, really. The name means 'toasted.' No, 'roasted.' Roasted in Roosteren." Behind the wheel, she gave a big laugh to her big joke, which I still don't get. Her English was impeccable, but her humor was . . .

I didn't know if she meant you'd have to be on drugs to live there, or in my new farmhouse.

When I think of Roosteren now, I think of the smell of roasted meat. Its char and fat. The warm steam pulled through the shards of flesh. In Dutch, the word for meat is "flesh." "Vlees." Which always seemed to me beautifully efficient. It doesn't matter if you are talking about pork or cold cuts, "flesh" is always present in any conversation where meat is. When I moved to the Netherlands, I was mostly vegetarian. I had been so on and off since I was twelve years old. I'd go back to eating meat when I "got hungry," which was my phrase for getting too anemic, or when I was offered it.

Like what happened when I was fourteen, and my family traveled to Pennsylvania and visited a German family. We were on a road trip to New York City and they were the mother and father of one of my mother's friends. They made us a white bean and pork stew, and I can still taste the softly caramelizing onions. But what I also taste is the bitter slap against my face when my mom heard me ask our hosts, "What's in it?" because at the time I wasn't "eating meat."

I don't think she slapped me actually; she rarely hit me. But she turned my wrist hard and took me into a hallway, where her words whispered, hissed, and spit. She gave me a speech about how arrogant it was to question any food that was put in front of me. Although I was serious about not eating meat because I loved animals, I also really loved people. And when the divide between the moral and immoral food no longer lined up as cleanly in my mind as humane vs. inhumane, what to eat stopped being a simple choice.

•

I met Marricka when I started volunteering at the refugee camp down the road from Roosteren, in an even more boring and less beautiful village. In Dutch, the word for those I'd call "refugees" is "asielzoekers," asylum seekers. I like this word better because it suggests that the people who live in asylum housing are looking for safety instead of running away from trouble.

But the place was bleak. Terrifying, actually. It would be over a year before I learned that the grounds had once been an insane asylum. The attendants often stopped by to dispense antipsychotics and antidepressants while I was visiting the rooms of one of the people who lived there, an experience that was uncomfortably public and impersonal. Once, turning the corner to the kitchen to say goodbye for the day to a man I knew, I found him hiding behind the door wielding a large, sharp carving knife. He'd received notice that he was being sent back to his country. When he saw me, he relaxed the knife in his fist as he set the knives in his eyes down.

"You could come to me and my husband's house," I said, at a loss for anything substantial I could do to help him. "We can make you food."

"Food? I don't need food," he said like he could have spit at me. "Vlees, vlees, vlees, that's all the Dutch ever do is eat." He ran away instead of waiting for the police to come and take him to the prison in Ter Apel, where all the unsuccessful asylum seekers were detained before they were deported. I saw him when he visited the camp again, some months later, healthily fed and well-dressed. He'd dated, impregnated, and married a Dutch woman; he could come and go as he pleased. He talked to a Dutch-nationalized man from the Republic of Congo, a former camp resident turned camp volunteer, who told me about him. "You know me . . . ," he said to him, "this is not the life I intended here . . ."

This is not the life I intended here . . . In my mind, the clause is still hanging. It feels like the statement is missing a "but," but what did he have to weigh on the other side of it?

Why had I offered him food, when I often feel the least at home in my body when deciding what to eat? Most meat doesn't feel at home there, but bone broth does and, occasionally, blood-rare steak. Then I worry about the parasites: what's eating off of me. But mostly I worry about what it means to say to someone else whether I do eat something, or don't. I think a lot about the large blue duck egg I consumed in its entirety at fifteen. It was a gift for Julie, a friend of mine who'd been tutoring a Chinese family in English at her college. They had invited her over for dinner. She had invited me.

They had selected that date for dinner because the egg was a delicacy and they had to wait, weeks I imagine, for it to arrive in the mail. It was congealed, speckled, and ultramarine. The egg's shell had dissolved in the preserving process; the shell being gone was probably what gave the egg its mottled blue color; the egg white was tender like thick gelatin. Our hosts cut the gelatinous egg into four pieces. Only the yolk, chalky and cerulean, stayed whole.

Julie was a picky eater, even by American standards. Her students kept encouraging her to try the egg, whose arrival they'd organized especially for her, but she refused. She would often complain, "It's the texture . . . ," picking at a piece of onion or mushroom when we ate lunch together. I knew when they began unpackaging the egg from its delicate box in front of her, when it came out its clear packaging pristine and unusual, that she'd never eat a piece. She took the small china saucer they'd presented her, with its piece of egg, and watched it jiggle. She tried to offer the egg back to our hosts, her students, to eat, but it was a present especially for her—they wouldn't touch it. She sniffed it, the nostrils turning up on her narrow, birdlike nose. Our hosts looked so excited. I noticed her nose twitch. "This smells funny," was the final judgment she'd make any time she refused to try something new.

I couldn't let her insult them. In the moment, that felt unpalatable.

So, I ate the entire thing. Finishing the egg slice Julie left idling on her plate for over two hours. I doubt it was meant to be consumed as a whole but rather as a side dish, as duck eggs are notoriously rich, and the taste was unfamiliar to me. I gagged through parts of it, and when dinner was finished, I nearly vomited, but in the stirs of my gut, I felt relief.

"Why did you do it?" Julie asked me, once we were back in her car. The uneasiness had subsided but I was still holding my stomach.

I couldn't let you hurt them, I wanted to say.

"I didn't want them to be hurt," I said, which didn't convey the meaning I was going for. I wanted her to feel the same food burden that I did—the knowledge that what you choose not to eat could hurt someone. There was privilege in her decision, yes, but also a keener sense of self-preservation. It would be decades before I learned the difference between what was good for me and what everyone else wanted of me. I was still in the midst of that reckoning when I moved to Roosteren and became a refugee camp volunteer.

Why did I work at the asylum seekers' center? Before arriving in the Netherlands and becoming a housewife, I was an architect in New York. It sounds glamorous, but I was unhappy.

I had gone to school, and had even interned at the Peggy Guggenheim Collection in Venice, Italy, in hopes of breaking into museum design. Instead, the best job I could find after getting my degree was with a firm that built jails.

Had we lived in Amsterdam, "somewhere more beautiful," I might have been able to find work with an English-speaking company, or even a Dutch architecture firm with a lot of American clients (since I didn't know the metric system, this was another language barrier to my practicing design in Europe). But we lived in Limburg, between the Belgian and German borders, decidedly rural and not particularly welcoming to dark-skinned English speakers.

People would mistake me for a refugee all the time. As someone running from. And they weren't kind about it. Cashiers at the grocery store would refuse to touch my hand to return my change, and drivers would yell at me if I parked in the wrong place because I couldn't read the posted sign. In the company of my husband, I was read a little differently, but not enough to make me feel welcome. I'd basically retreated inside.

But once I was done freeing the bird out our bedroom window and ironing my husband's extensive collection of dress shirts, the weeks passed by with nothing real to do. I wanted to contribute something. One of Kees' friends suggested volunteering. In my mind, there wasn't much that I could do for people seeking asylum since I didn't speak Dutch. But I occasionally had a car and many of the foreigners spoke English, and the fact that I was just as foreign as they were might provide a different level of comfort. I strived not to give the impression that their world tasted funny to me.

•

Some months into my volunteering, Marricka and I are driving on the road back to Roosteren. She cracks jokes I don't respond to. We got into a fight over a DVD player. And the fact that she, now, attempts to cover over the frustration of just a few minutes before with small talk irritates me. I try to keep my anger at bay by not answering her, letting the awkwardness steam and release like hot cake. But she, in her own discomfort, keeps rattling on, and I can feel my anger boiling over.

I cared about Marricka. I felt a lot of gratitude for her taking me under her wing when I was so new to town, the generosity of her rides to work, the patience with which she spoke to me exclusively in English. She had this way I appreciated, of bridging the gap between herself and other people by considering how she would feel in their situation, a true empathy. When I offered her money or suggested I pick her up when I was able, she would brush it off, saying, "You two are just starting out, I remember how that was when my husband and I were your age," or "It's on my way, and anyway, there's no reason for you to waste petrol when the price is this high."

For the most part, she treated the women we visited in the asylum the same way. She approached their circumstances with understanding, not pity, and rarely talked down to any of them, which is why I was surprised that a conversation over some home videos would lead to such a big brawl.

"It's too bad you don't have a DVD player," said Marricka to BabyMay, a young new mother from Sierra Leone. "You know, if you did, I could bring you old Baby Genius videos for your baby to watch." Her baby was only a few weeks old and we were bringing supplies, infant diapers, and a secondhand car seat Marricka had used for her grandson.

"You know, it is very important to start developing a child's brain at an early age," Marricka said to the woman, her voice grave and serious. She was holding BabyMay's newborn. I watched the new mother do the calculus for how she might procure a DVD player. I shot Marricka a look that suggested she take that obligation out of the conversation's air, but she was busy playing with the newborn's tiny fingers.

We were meant to take BabyMay and her infant to a doctor's appointment, then the grocery store. The weekly stipend each asylum center resident received from the government was substantial enough to cover basic living expenses, but as with any fixed income, the asylum seekers had to be smart about making the money stretch, often purchasing things like clothes, dishware, and baby strollers from the kringloopwinkel—the Dutch secondhand store. A working DVD player wasn't a likely thing to find at a secondhand shop. In order for Baby-May to take advantage of Marricka's offer, she'd have to buy one new.

Marricka seemed oblivious to the fact BabyMay returned to her car that day with one small bag of groceries—powdered baby formula and some bottles of Ensure—but I noticed it. BabyMay would fast so that she could afford the DVD player. I knew this. I tried to explain this to Marricka as we sat in the asylum parking lot after we dropped BabyMay off.

"That's ridiculous," Marricka said. "She's a smart girl. She'd never starve herself for a DVD player."

She wasn't "starving" herself. BabyMay had made clear on many occasions that she would fast as a spiritual practice to cleanse herself or focus her energy. Having someone in authority tell her a DVD player was an essential tool for her infant's enlightenment meant she would make the sacrifice of food to save her son. I tried to explain.

"She would if a white woman, a successful mother—a missionary of sorts—told her it's the best way for her to educate her child in Europe." I was hoping maybe the parallels between our work, ministry, and colonization might strike a chord with her. But she instead found this more confusing.

"Who would think—? I didn't say that. I just offered to bring her some old DVDs—"

"If she had a DVD player, which she didn't," I said. My patience was thinning. And so was hers. Marricka let out an

exasperated sigh, the one my mother-in-law often used to pa-
tronize my Americanness.

"Well, how is that my fault?" She turned over the engine
and backed out the parking lot, commencing the small talk
that would carry us the whole way home and continued to
piss me off.

Before moving to the Netherlands, I'd thought little about
white privilege. To be clear, I thought a whole lot about
racism—c'mon, I grew up in Kentucky. But I was a round-the-
way girl from Harlem in 2010. I wanted a husband and children. I had no aspirations of being political, or a college
professor, back then. I brushed off my family's concern about
moving to "the same country that sold our ancestors into slavery" as hyperbolic and unprogressive. I brushed off Kees'
friends who said, as a new Dutch fiancée, I should take down
the Facebook profile pic of me in a "Black Is Beautiful" T-shirt
from the Studio Museum, because it was too "Black Power."

I drew the line at the Dutch still celebrating Christmas in
blackface. But, before we got married, Kees and I had already
negotiated that I would never have to witness it, vowing I
would always go home to the States during that time. We kept
that arrangement, but it was ignorant of me to assume I could
avoid discrimination by avoiding the Netherlands at a certain
time of year—a sad consequence of my own social privilege,

believing there was racism I had control over and considering that kind of racism benign.

Back in 2010, the Dutch didn't have a special phrase for "white privilege," and even today, from what I understand, they just use ours. But what I learned about in the Netherlands wasn't "white privilege," exactly. What I learned about was something bigger, older, and adjacent—very much like how the more Dutch words I memorized the easier it was for me to understand German, Dutch being, for the most part, very old German. Very old white privilege is what I like to call white aggrandizement, because "aggrandizement" is something the Dutch do have a word for. "Verheerlijking," a cousin of the noun "vergroting," which can mean "magnification," "amplification," or "enlargement."

My husband would sometimes say "verheerlijking" in Maastricht dialect to insult the type of man who liked to stick his paunch stomach into things and tell him what to do, so I would sometimes joke to myself that the phrase would be "too big for your britches" in Kentuckian. In Dutch, the prefix "ver" can mean a lot of things, but it often indicates the degree of something, in the sense of making, causing, or bringing into being. Aggrandizement is more powerful than privilege. More useful in describing what I was seeing. "Privilege" may be thought of as something inherited, that someone passively has but can make a choice about abusing. "Aggrandizement" is active, an advantaged person's inflated sense of worth compared to others. How would I translate "verheerlijking" in English? *Imperialism just hits differently.*

It wasn't lost on me that the Dutch were responsible for the exploitation of our resources and people throughout West Africa and South Asia, the boats that brought our ancestors to the Americas and the Caribbean. As a lit professor, I taught *Zong!* by M. NourbeSe Philip, a book of erasure poems built from the court case files of a slave ship. On one ruthless, infamous voyage, the captain of the *Zong* got lost and threw the captured Africans overboard, calculating that if they died at sea he could claim more from the insurance money than he would for a ship filled with starved and dehydrated people. The insurance case went to court to decide whether or not the captain was guilty of murder or property damage, for the dispersing of valuable "cargo."

It's only been a few decades since the Dutch were overtly involved in any colonizing or war efforts. If you trace back Dutch wealth today, the money they are so proud of investing in social healthcare systems and an open border system of political asylum, you're likely to bump smack into the aggrandizement that makes them ignore why so many people need political asylum to begin with.

The Dutch have removed all sense of racial and ethnic bias from the ways they tell their history. Instead, they've crafted a version of their mercantilism that was opportunistic, but only profited from other whites' biases against nonwhites. They didn't create "privilege," only its supply chain.

BabyMay had been a flight attendant in Sierra Leone. She'd been living in the Netherlands on an expired passport after she met on Facebook a man she thought she was going to marry. She'd been having a pretty grand time being expatriate and cosmopolitan until she tripped down a flight of stairs in a pair of stilettos. She broke her leg in three places. When she went to the hospital, she showed up in the system as illegal. Her options were deportation or asylum. When she was booked into the asylum, she found out she was pregnant. Her boyfriend had already stopped returning her phone calls. It was nearly a year after her son was born that I'd gained Baby-May's trust enough for her to tell me this, showing me pictures of her saying goodbye to her coworkers and her mother. And the pictures during her first months in Europe filled with glitter, heels, and bodycon dresses, like any twentysomething out on the town in a brilliant new life.

The first day I met her, she'd just arrived at the asylum— shell-shocked, pregnant, her leg in a full-length cast. The day her son was born Marricka was the first person BabyMay called for help with all the foreign nurses and paperwork. Marricka waited at the hospital all day for the infant to be born, and for his father to arrive to claim the child as his own, as a Dutch citizen—which he never did.

A week after our argument, Marricka and I returned to the asylum center. BabyMay had a DVD player resting on her mantel with a doily placed underneath and the dust cover stickers still on. I noticed it. I asked her to tell Marricka why she bought the brand-new device.

"Because you told me you'd bring me DVDs for my son," BabyMay said. Marricka wasn't hearing it.

"BabyMay, tell her I didn't tell you to buy the DVD player," Marricka responded. "You know that isn't true."

"But you did," BabyMay said flatly. "You told me I needed one, and so I bought it."

It went on like that for a while, Marricka laughing, and needling, trying to intimidate BabyMay into giving another answer, but she had no reason to change her story.

"Maybe you misunderstood," Marricka said finally. She never apologized.

We returned to Marricka's car much later that afternoon after visiting a few more residents. I'd had it, and when we opened the car doors the Roosteren summer heat sliced through us like a knife through cake. I tried one more time to get Marricka to admit what she did to BabyMay was wrong so that she wouldn't make the same mistake again, but she refused.

"You refuse to see it because you're racist," I said. I didn't yet know the word "verheerlijken."

Marricka yelled at me and beat on the hood of the car, working herself into tears.

"I'm not racist!" she screamed, and banged her keys on the car hood. I don't know how I'd expected her to take that, but now I knew I had to calm her down.

"Look, I'm racist too," I said. "Racist" wasn't what I meant. What I wanted to say to Marricka was that I'm also learning the ways my privilege biases me against people. The privileges of being American. The privileges of being married to a Dutchman. The privileges of being middle class. Just as I didn't speak any Dutch, in 2010 I hadn't yet learned the vocabulary for talking about things like "unconscious bias," "white privilege," or even "white saviorism." The Netherlands was my first language lesson. It was an education. The rest was still to come.

"We all have blind spots for the prejudices we hold for other people . . . ," I said. Marricka was the first friend I'd made in the Netherlands. *Instead of shutting down, maybe it's better to open up*, I thought. "After living in Harlem, I had to teach myself to be less prejudiced against Puerto Ricans," I shared as a peace offering. I looked up at Marricka; she looked confused. "New York," I said, "Harlem, New York." She thought I'd meant Haarlem—the Netherlands—and she was trying to calculate how the Puerto Ricans and I got there.

"What was your problem with Puerto Ricans?" she asked, dabbing her wet eyes with a cloth as she slid behind the steering wheel. It was a ramshackle thing that I blurted out in the heat of the moment. I buckled my seat belt and began to answer her but couldn't. You know how, sometimes, you yell out things in an argument that involve more unpacking than you have the energy for? But I can do that unpacking now, for you, because I recognize the impulse was my attempt at greater intimacy between us.

Back in Harlem, before I moved, I was having dinner at a restaurant with a friend to celebrate my engagement, and we were leaving when a white Puerto Rican man grabbed my arm to tell me he didn't like the way I looked in my glasses.

"What's the word for being racist against nerds?" he asked me. "I'm racist against nerds."

I was scared by how he looked at me—in all likelihood, he was just plain racist—but I made it into a joke so I could brush it off. After that run-in, my friends and I would use the term "racist" to apply to anything we felt an aversion toward. Racist against carbs. Racist against non-Manhattan New York area codes. The absurdity took the sting out of being young and Black in the early Obama years when we were seeing images of a First Black Family everywhere in a world that had become no safer for us.

I was prejudiced against the ways I'd seen lighter-skinned Puerto Ricans rudely treat darker-skinned Puerto Ricans,

African Americans, and Afro-Latino people of various ethnicities. The nerd-racist remark had just been the tipping point.

Now I was bringing the language of my frustrations in America into this conversation with Marricka because, despite her privilege and our arguing, I'd started to feel close to her—like a family member, like an old friend. I was trying to explain to her that I too wanted to rid myself of bias, any of it against any group of people, that I based on a stereotype. I used the word "racist," in the moment, as a point of connection, but it wasn't quite right, as I struggled to find my way.

I didn't have the energy to say all that, then. "Well, as long as you are racist too," Marricka said when I just sighed in response. She put her sunglasses on and her foot on the gas.

I went for weeks without seeing Marricka after that. I spent most of my time at home crying under the covers in bed. I told my husband repeatedly that I didn't think I could do this, that I didn't think I could make it in this country where I felt misunderstood so deeply and so regularly. In the midst of my depression, Marricka called, inviting us to her family's house for dinner that weekend.

"You need to give her a chance, she's just an old-country woman," my husband said.

"She's only eight years older than me, and chooses to advocate for very vulnerable people," I said to him. But I did feel bonded to Marricka on the level of our both being small-town girls who turned into women who could stick a big, whopping foot in their mouths. Truth be told, so often, the things she said and did that cut me deeply were not unlike the stuff I'd grown accustomed to accepting from straight-shooting conservative Kentuckians. The difference was the space she occupied, as a volunteer emissary, as an agent of change, as the emergency contact of so many people of color in crisis. As the only Black woman who volunteered at the center, I couldn't be silent. But I wasn't opposed to reconciling.

We pulled up to her house around three o'clock on a Sunday afternoon. It was our first time visiting. The gardens were neat but not overly manicured. The inside of the house was energetic and cozy, gezellig.

"May I get you a Coke?" offered her preteen daughter. Both she and her teenage brother were cheery and thoughtful. My husband and Marricka's son played football in the back while I helped her cut cantaloupe. She talked about her husband's alcoholism and depression. He had just come in to shake my hand and tell me a banana-themed knock-knock joke before going back to his study to finish some client work. He was now three years sober, but Marricka confessed the difficulty of the time had driven away their oldest daughter who had run off, gotten married, had a baby, and divorced just a few years ago, all by the age of nineteen. Marricka looked deeply sad. I understood how volunteering at the center made her feel she might have the chance to help someone else young and impressionable. Like BabyMay. Like myself. I wanted to like her, but my hard feelings stuck like an egg in the back of my throat.

For dinner, she was preparing this stew the Dutch kept calling "chili con carne." I'd had it a few times during dinner invitations, including at my in-laws' house, as if the one recipe were making the rounds through South Limburg, or perhaps everyone did it to be hospitable—to give me something "American" to eat. But it wasn't chili as I was used to at home: spicy and humble over rice or, in Kentucky and Ohio and around there, nutmegged and piled high with shredded cheese on top of spaghetti. The sauce included no chilies of any kind. It was a can of diced tomatoes to which Marricka added water to stretch and then squeezed in ketchup to thicken. Next, she threw in some chopped pieces of colored bell pepper. While the bells sweat in their stew pot, Marricka removed a block of ground beef from its packaging.

"This is really the only kind of meat I can eat," she said, resigned and proud. "I just can't deal with it when it looks too much like an animal." She took a jar of smoked paprika out the cabinets and sprinkled the amount I would use to garnish potato salad on the meat. She broke up the meat with a spatula, but only a little bit—the pieces still sizzling in the pan like worms. I wanted to grab the spatula, a few spices out the cabinets, and pound the flesh until it looked like the ground beef that I was used to; the strange serpentine curves looked to me like intestines. But Marricka was my host. And so, into the hot watery broth I watched the worms go. She stirred all the ingredients around together, once, before plating it with fresh rolls. Thank god she didn't try to make corn bread.

We all sat down to eat. The broth was bitter and scalding. The skins of the undercooked bell peppers speared my tongue as the flavorless worms floated between them.

"Yum, this is delicious. Marricka, thank you," my husband said, scooping the stew and the bread in his mouth for a sturdy bite. This was the training his family had offered up to him as a young boy, whoever the host: always compliment the food.

●

Of course the night couldn't end kindly. I finished my bowl of vlees and turned down a second saying that we really should be going since her husband still had work to finish for the morning and we didn't want to impose, but the family invited us to stay for a movie and dessert. They'd rented *August Rush*. Terrence Howard showed up on-screen.

"You know, I just don't trust Black men with light eyes," she said to all of us. "They just look shifty, don't they?" she asked me. I dug my nails into the chair's armrest. My husband looked at me apologetically. I wanted to laugh, amid my pent-up anger and the absurdity of it, but I swallowed it down and stayed silent.

●

Months later, Marricka and I are standing in a slaughter-house. I've borrowed my husband's car and together we bus a half-dozen asylum seekers to a centuries-old operation in town that sells the freshest, cheapest meats. It's where the local butcher shops pick up their cuts before turning each over into the sanitized folios I am used to purchasing from the grocery store three steps down the supply chain.

A cow hangs from the rafters freshly skinned and opened. From it, visitors select the choicest cuts for the meals they plan to cook that week and the attendant, in a black rubber apron and white cloak, harvests those pieces from the long body, placing them in butcher paper for the customers to inspect before they make their purchases. Jebbeh was next in line.

This feels just like home, Jebbeh said to me as she looked around the slaughter room. She made her selections with the attendant and bounced her knees to keep her infant son, one of her two twins, asleep while he rested in a wrap on her back. Jebbeh was Liberian. She'd fled her home after her twin sister was murdered for being one of only two uncircumcised women in her village. Jebbeh's mother had been the village's midwife; she didn't want to subject her daughters to the health risks of circumcision and, since she carried a high position, was able to keep the girls protected, until she unexpectedly died. First, they cut slits across the twins' skin and slipped a material into the wounds so that as the wounds healed, subcutaneous markings formed and would never leave, alerting the rest of the villagers to the girls' "unclean" status. Young women by now, but without their mother as a family head, this sign of their uncircumcision opened the girls' doors to multiple rapes. Jebbeh's sister couldn't stand it anymore. She agreed to let the village leaders circumcise her, to end the ostracism. They took her into the procedural tent while Jebbeh waited outside, and they murdered her.

Jebbeh ran. While living in the forest, she met a woodsman who protected her and later became the father of her own twins. They wanted to get married but the marks on Jebbeh's skin advertised her past in a way they couldn't hide forever. He procured a way to get her to France while pregnant, Jebbeh dressed as the secretary of a diplomat, carrying fake visa papers. She was meant to go to the embassy and plead for asylum as soon as the plane landed. But, with limited French, she lost her way, ended up in the streets, and encountered another Liberian woman—an auntie—who claimed she would help Jebbeh find someplace safe. She sold Jebbeh to traffickers. They brought her to the Netherlands to work in a brothel. She ran away once more and ended up in prison, then, finally, the asylum center—where her two children were born.

When Jebbeh said the slaughterhouse reminded her of home, she looked whole. All of the center residents who came with Marricka and me that day preferred shopping along the village's main street instead of at the large chain grocery store because the experience of food was personal, not clinical. In some ways this was a homecoming. Jebbeh had learned enough Dutch to haggle with the attendant, a surly man with a goitered face. Jebbeh's insistence that he could give her a better price for cow flesh, as she shifted her waking son from her back to her hip, made him smile. He always threw in extra rib bones for her. "A mother needs meat," he said, in slow English, as he handed her the white-wrapped beef in a white bag. I stepped back from beneath the cut cow to take in the whole scene. The slaughterhouse was beautiful. Like a Francis Bacon painting I might have stood in front of for hours, years earlier, when I worked at the Peggy Guggenheim Collection. The building was cathedral height and stone. All the blood had stained the stone the color of bricks in rain, its spatter patterning the walls as if, at dinner, all the guests had thrown their wineglasses to end a party—the end effect ironic, macabre, and joyful. The joy surprised me, but I felt it innately. The movement of the spirit and the human body. The transference of the life of the cow into ours. I was in awe of what I witnessed. I said a blessing for the cow's sacrifice. I thanked her. Before that, I had only thanked God for food. "It's disgusting, isn't it?" said Marricka. She carried Jebbeh's daughter on her shoulder. She seemed pleased by her observation, she wanted me to commiserate, she thought she'd been able to read my mind.

"Eh," I said. Neutral and noncommittal. I hoped she'd move on. I hoped she wouldn't call the place "savage" in front of all of our friends.

"Savage, really," she said as she moved the baby to her hip, rocking her gently. She repeated her feelings on the benefits of ground chuck and packaged meats.

It was obvious, given the size of Jebbeh's slaughterhouse haul, that she intended to cook a meal to thank us. We helped her bring her groceries and twin car seats back into her room at the center.

"Laten we een afspraak maken," Jebbeh said, practicing her Dutch. We made plans to come back in the afternoon, two days later. I told Jebbeh how insanely excited I was. West African food has been my favorite since I was a baby. When I was born, my mother's best friend was Ghanaian and she often watched me. Even now, she jokes about how I'd beg for "peanut butter" soup with a pacifier in my mouth. Jebbeh knew my favorite dish was a fish stew made with either spinach or cassava leaves. Marricka too was getting excited as we described the food, imagining the fragrant stain of palm oil on our teeth. But the thought of Marricka coming to eat Liberian food was stressing me, my stomach grumbling with hunger and pleasure as it twisted into knots.

"It's not a typical Dutch stew," I tried to explain to Marricka in the parking lot between our cars. She felt I was—and I was—being patronizing.

"Yes, yes, I know that." She claimed she'd eaten plenty of African dishes at potlucks for her church group. I'd been to some—it was an easy place to meet other Pan-African English speakers—and the dishes were usually dress-up revamps of colonial favorites, like a peanut soup that was essentially "chili con carne" with peanut butter added. No spice. The ground beef replaced with chuck roast.

Jebbeh was on her way to becoming a "Nederlands vrouw," as she called it, but cooked all her recipes just as she remembered them. On the day of Jebbeh's dinner invitation, Jebbeh was finishing up her table arrangement by making comfortable seats of the twin beds arranged on either side of her room. She'd borrowed porcelain plates and bowls from the Persian family a few rooms down, who sought asylum to protect their daughters from becoming the "brides" of Iranian soldiers. I recognized the plates because the family would often use them to offer us biscuits and tea. Jebbeh had placed the twins in their car seats to make room for us. She had placed her television on the floor and moved the heavy dresser it usually sat upon from the wall to the middle of the floor to create a table on which we could serve ourselves. From little more than a hot plate, she'd made us cassava-leaf stew and jollof rice. In her Instant Pot, she was still cooking the fresh white rice to put the stew on top of. The bell dinged, and she began plating the food in china bowls, the lid of each pot thick with steam.

"This tastes like home," I told Jebbeh. I'd set the serving plate down on the bed and was holding the bowl of stew in my hands. I used the spoon to mix the sticky rice further through the gritty fat in the stew. "I wish we had fufu," I said, "so this would be easier to eat with our hands."

"You know fufu as well," she said. "Ah! You are a Liberian woman."

"Maybe we're related," I said, slipping a little into my Kentucky drawl. We hadn't even started into the jollof rice. "Can I have another bowl of stew first?" I asked our host, and she waved to me like the madam of a fancy house.

"You are welcome. Help yourself."

Across from me, Marricka was struggling. I'd eaten a lot, and fast, because inside Jebbeh's food I found happiness—but also to distract her because I knew Marricka was gearing up to be rude and that she wouldn't stop herself.

This tastes like worms in water, I still wanted to say about that chili con carne of hers I'd shoveled down months earlier, its memory still awful in my mouth. But I didn't.

"What is this?" Marricka asked after she'd poked at the plate and bowl until it turned lukewarm.

"It's stew, Marricka. Remember? Just as we talked about," I said. My tone was loud and obvious. I wanted her to notice, and Jebbeh to know, I had tried to prep her for this moment.

Marricka looked up at me like a dead-eyed fish. In the stew were the beef tips Jebbeh bought from the cow I blessed, but also hunks of smoked whitefish still on the bone, dried and crushed shrimp, cassava leaf, garlic, onions, spices, and small pieces of tripe. Aside from the beef, the meat was used mostly as seasoning. I'd prayed into the thick paste of palm oil and cassava leaves, which painted everything in the dish like a verdant pesto, hoping that Marricka would pick through the bites she thought she could manage and leave what she wouldn't eat just to try it, just to be hospitable. But Marricka wasn't having it. She had acted so honored that Jebbeh had asked us to her home to sit down and be served, but in the presence of the food itself, she was full of fear and slight on social graces. It hadn't really occurred to me that the early lesson I'd learned of my obligation to the food that was in front of me was as cosmopolitan as it was cultural.

Learning to adjust to food so early in my life was my first lesson in traveling. I learned not only to eat the blue egg. Over time, I learned to savor it, to crave it, to adopt it as my inheritance. I cherish this kind of privilege. A worldliness that is one of the overlooked advantages of traveling in my body. I have had to adapt to so much in the world that is foreign to me. The fluidity I've developed because of this brings me closer to a world that is beautiful, delicious. I am no longer the ugly tourist with demands that the world conform to my palate. Marricka might never feel this. In the same way that I'll never have the luxury of agonizing over a plate of meat and greens as if they might hurt me. I am lucky. I live in the freedom of finding no terror in another person's mundane.

Violence. That's what I'm afraid of. The possibility that my Black femininity will render in someone the desire to cause menace to me or someone I care about. Like the man wielding a meat cleaver in the asylum kitchen in a desperate attempt to protect himself from immigration jail. Like the body of Baby-May's father—a journalist—whom she saw as a teenage girl hung and lit on fire in front of her house because he spoke out against Sierra Leone's colonialist government. Like the scars forced onto Jebbeh's forearms, the way they mark her intact clitoris as an invitation for destruction. Like the man who cornered me with his white Saab on my way home from the bus in Roosteren, because he assumed—by virtue of my skin color and English accent—that I must be a prostitute. I cannot be scared of the cut, fat, and taste of another animal. Vlees. Vlees. If you hand me a bowl, I'll eat it because I have far too much else on my mind to worry about.

"What's this?" Marricka asked Jebbeh, pointing to a small slice of intestine. Jebbeh couldn't think of the word in either Dutch or English.

"It's just fat," I said, my mouth green and full.

"It's our stew," Jebbeh said, lifting the lid to the pot like in an instructional video, turning the ladle to show Marricka each facet of the meal, the same way shaking hands with a new person was a gesture to show we were free from weapons. "This piece has just a little bit of beef and fish, please try it." She offered Marricka a tea saucer of food, taking back the bowl Marricka had messed over. Marricka took it to her lips and sniffed it.

"No, I can't eat this," she said. "It's too gross." As if Jebbeh and I weren't there. As her vision panned out from the small plate, she must have remembered.

"I'm sorry," Marricka said, "I'm a vegetarian."

Since when? I wanted to ask, and so did Jebbeh, but she managed the situation more elegantly.

"I guess you won't want to try the jollof," she said, presenting it to Marricka, the top dressed in roasted chicken legs.

"Well, I can have a little bit of that," she said. Jebbeh scooped the jollof onto a plate. "But just the rice." Marricka covered the plate with her hand to make sure no chicken was added.

Marricka picked at a few grains of the seasoned rice before I made up an appointment and announced it was time for us to leave. Her eyes were still glazed but she bit at that small morsel of mercy.

"What a pity, we must be going," she said. She reached out

to shake Jebbeh's hand but then opted for an awkward hug. She picked up each of the babies and kissed them on the cheeks.

"Thank you," I said as Jebbeh and I hugged. "Thank you so much." I held her arms in my hands. I asked if I could borrow some Tupperware to take the jollof home, "for my husband." She winked and packaged it, slapping my right buttock. She handed it to me in a grocery bag. As we gathered our coats, Jebbeh began cleaning. We waved our last goodbyes and as we walked out I saw Jebbeh take a big spoonful of Marricka's untouched stew and eat it, before throwing the bowl full of food into the sink.

Outside the asylum center, Marricka looks relieved, if not pleased with herself, that she turned down Jebbeh's meal.

"I don't know how you could stomach it," she says, holding her own, "all those meats mixed together . . . it looked so unsanitary."

"It's my favorite cuisine," I answer, using this French word I never say to guide her toward some European diplomacy. I want her to drop the subject.

"Still," she says, "I can't stomach that much meat."

In my mind, I compress the scene so that this is the day she pulls a speck and cheese on a roll from a sandwich bag stuffed in her purse, but I'm sure it isn't. I just remember that within the time that followed—a few days or weeks—that moment appeared, the raw bacon hanging from her mouth the same color as Dutch flesh, and I knew I couldn't stomach her anymore.

●

I kept going to the asielzoekers center for a year after that, but with much less frequency. I met other expat wives who volunteered and joined them. I ran into Marricka occasionally but she too was coming by irregularly. Jebbeh and her twins were granted asylum and given a house in the country, near Rotterdam. BabyMay and her toddler were sent to prison in Ter Appel, where a lawyer fought her imprisonment and impending deportation as a human rights violation—the courts decided in her favor and granted them both citizenship. I visited them each, once, in their new homes, to bring them gifts and say goodbye.

It was fall again when I visited the center for the last time. I took a new friend with me, a woman who'd been a lawyer at home in the Philippines but did nothing for work now since her husband was quite rich. We pulled up in her Mercedes. The air was thick, like a smokehouse, the bricks covered in a layer of brine that crinkled like roasted meat. We walked from the parking lot. Yellow caution tape circled the grounds all around the perimeter. We were not permitted entry. Diggy, a dreadlocked Eritrean refugee I'd known for over a year now but whose story I did not know, stepped as close as he could from across the band of tape.

"He killed himself," Diggy said. He spoke a name I didn't know. "They were going to send him back today, and so he stood right there, covered himself in a can of gasoline, and lit himself on fire." The space Diggy pointed to was slight. Like the starburst of a shadow. As pungent as the air was, there was no clear sign that a man in flames had ever stood there. I held on to the flimsy yellow tape for support. I thought I was going to shit myself. My friend unclasped her Prada bag and covered her mouth with a napkin. *We are breathing him in*, I thought, *we are consuming what is left of him*. But he hadn't died.

Another resident stepped up toward us. He was lank with tufts of gray hair growing in patches around his temples. He paced and flailed his arms. I couldn't understand his accent. I'd seen him around but he always seemed this agitated, so I had avoided him—a privilege of mine. Diggy was trying to explain that an ambulance had taken the burned man to the hospital. The tall man talked over him.

"Man," he said, in a raspy voice, "if it was me, I would have started from the feet. That's what he did wrong, man." He play-punched Diggy in the ribs. "He did it wrong. His hair just set ablaze, man. POOF!" He lifted his fingers in the air and blew at them like a dandelion bud. "Go for the feet, I told him, go for the feet."

It would take me years to work through everything I saw in Roosteren. The time was shocking, and painful, and hard to digest. Long after we moved to another town, I'd have dreams where the scent of burning flesh wafted in the air outside the asylum and the caution tape pulled from it spikes like meat from bones. In my privilege, I had always assumed that the refugee process was a troubled but essential part of giving equity to human life. Even now, I don't know enough to speak on it really. But you know what I feel? There's a troubling aggrandizement to believing we can heal the damage we have wrought dividing our borders and waging imperialism. As an American, I am still a privileged benefactor of this system. African American or not. And though I am thankful for an education that did not close me off to the delicacies of other cultures, I wonder who I'd be now if I had not seen firsthand, as a foreigner, what it means to seek refuge in a foreign country.

●

The burn victim lived through the autumn. It was a nightly report on the news alongside stories where reporters asked notable Dutch people—politicians, human rights workers, sex workers turned celebrities—if the asylum system in the Netherlands was a crisis that needed to be solved.

By December, the story of the deceased had grown stale and the air unbearably icy. We'd moved from the barn without screens to a cottage just outside of Heerlen. I knit while my husband and I watched Dutch late-night television. I mostly zoned out, until I got the premise: two men were about to eat each other on live television. The talk show topic of the evening, cannibalism. The show had teased about the event for months; no one, it seemed, stopped to consider if the timing of the stunt was tasteless. The two hosts had pieces of meat surgically removed from their bodies so that the other could testify to what a human tastes like. *Vlees, vlees vlees,* they say. That word I understand. The two hosts sniff the small bags of their meat and a chef weighs in, as a flesh expert.

The scene is strange. In the background, two dancers dressed in pantyhose and *Penthouse* corsets take seats on the steps of the set while the show's presenters lean in their tailored suits toward the open flames of a gas stove. They watch the chef place the small morsels into hot oil. They sizzle and pink like cubes of bacon. Whether the TV broadcast is meant to be ironic, macabre, or sophisticated, I couldn't tell you. Dutch entertainment likes to play on all three. While they cook, one of the hosts is wide-eyed. He looks like he has tears in his eyes. But once the meat is cooked, everyone gets dressed like it's after eight, and they lay out white linens, candelabras, and china, just to eat each other.

"Verheerlijking," I say to myself as they spear in their forks and sniff at their roasted bodies. *This is how they slaughter us. This is it,* I think.

On Intimacy

Kyoto is molecular. A city of the mind. That's one of the things that made it easy for me to fall in love with. You don't have to know what to not pay attention to. A map is a nudge. The city's journey is meant to be intuitive. Thoughtful. This intimacy is rewarding. Like interactive theater. The more you get lost, the more you're likely to find exactly what you're looking for.

It was a city I never intended to visit. A friend of mine whom I was visiting in China suggested it would be a good week's getaway since the sky was so polluted in Shanghai it was too dangerous to go outside. And after a seventeen-hour flight it seemed a shame to stay inside.

My friend was an excellent tour guide. After a few days she'd planned for mulling quietly through a traditional tea service and Shinto temples, she took us to an evening performance at a Butoh theater. Butoh is an experience unlike anything I've ever witnessed. Another superlative, both earned. Butoh opened me up to Kyoto and, in turn, the city opened itself to me, leaving me with the feeling of being close. Connected. The Butoh theater was a small, two-story house nestled between concrete office and apartment blocks. Our showing was ten p.m., late enough at night where the rows of modest businesses were closing tight, shop owners pouring steaming buckets of water on the sidewalk to brush away the day's refuse. Across the street, the few apartment lights scattered like teeth, leaving a slightly checkered illumination on the theater's long sidewalk, dressed on either side by garden pebbles. One rose petal had been placed on each step leading up to the house. A sign in multiple languages encouraged us to walk the path in silence, to take in the ambience. Everything felt a little bit gray, like film noir, making the edges of the red-petaled rose that much more seductive.

Once we entered the house a midfifties woman in a bleached cotton kimono handed us a one-page stage program. We were ushered into the onetime living room through a narrow hallway.

Only six seats. Only six, the number of people the show could entertain at a time. Only one of the patrons was Japanese—all of us looked like travelers. The seats were small wooden blocks with a cushion set perilously atop them, which I struggled to balance on while reading the English program.

I took a breath and grounded myself. The butter-yellow paper explained that the woman who handed us the programs was an actor in the show. The program explained that she was new to Butoh, having only practiced it about thirty years. I turned to my friend and pointed to that part of the program. We were both writers; it sounded intriguing, refreshing even, to think that after thirty years of practicing art, I could still be in my infancy. We commented on the difference, the pressure to succeed young.

To succeed young in life in America, as if your earliest contributions are always meant to be the longest lasting. I wonder what the actor studied before or in addition to Butoh and what its "newness" felt like to her. The freedom to be given decades of discovery.

"If she's a newbie, I wonder what a master looks like," I said to my friend. The program furnished an answer: the second actor in that night's performance was a Butoh performer in his eighties.

The house lights dimmed. There was music—more, moaning—and the actor in the bleached kimono walked into the stage room carrying a few dried rosebuds and seated herself uncomfortably in the corner. A rag doll, her eyes slits, as if she were dead. But I prefer to think of her as dreaming. I liked thinking that the second actor who would later enter the stage was a projection of her consciousness.

Her back was leaned against the wall, slouched, her legs

straight out and held at an awkward angle. I marveled at her as she maintained that same fixed position for the entirety of the performance, her face serene, her body immobile, her shoulder nestled in the corner of the living room; the show lasted forty-five minutes.

●

There is little that I want more than to be close—there are ways I feel the absence of closeness has actually paralyzed me. Something I used to be good at when I traveled frequently was fast, short rapports. It allowed me to be an incredible adventurer and, likely, a terrible long-term lover. I think this is a feeling more and more of us understand. In the culture we live in, intimacies are abundant but intimacy is scarce. Sex, social contact, information. It's easy for us to get what we want, but not want what we need—to be close to each other. It's not excitement we need, but the nearness of it.

What do I love about intimacy? The assurance that when I am no longer here, I will not be something easily left behind. The possibility there is something in me that is easy to see into, to adhere back to. I love theater because it's the place where I notice my most intimate parts. My joy in the face of such vulnerability resonates; I'm always the person stand-up comics look to to finish a bit or whom a magician pulls onstage to be an accomplice. Art has always been kind and sees me.

In one of my favorite stories where I function as its love interest, I'm visiting the interactive Manhattan play *Sleep No More*, a film noir version of *Macbeth*. It's got several secret personal performances. I didn't know this. The stage is an entire hotel. Everyone except the cast is masked. And alone, digging for that seed pod within the world, and of the show's several secrets, I unearthed three private ones: actors who took me in small rooms and fed me tea from spoons, or whispered a moving monologue in my ear that I was worthy of beauty and enlightenment. Exquisite. It was useful. The taking care, taking time, was exactly how I wanted to see my life. Straight as the light that refracts from the edges of glass. Looking into the edge of what we humanly feel instead of grazing its outline. At the places I break, light shines through. A falling in love of the mind.

Butoh is a type of theater that became popular in Japan around 1959. The program linked its origins to the bombing of Hiroshima. Compared to Kabuki theater, which is usually distanced and heavily costumed and ornate, Butoh is a theater of stark closeness. It involves very controlled articulations of the body, throughout the body, often on sets that are made out of the remnants of something else, like abandoned houses or sidewalks. It is a theater of what's left. I meditated greatly on its connection to the war—particularly the atomic bomb. Butoh actors often perform with a film of white paint covering their entire bodies and making grotesque facial expressions.

It's impossible for me not to flicker through the photographs I remember seeing of the bombing during my childhood, so overbearingly frightening, and see the art that has arisen from them. Butoh's bold pain is building from the residual. Most of us never want to get to that part of intimacy. Guttural, overwhelming vulnerability. It's not a game for the young; when we're young, we're figuring out how well we can advertise ourselves, and when we're old, most of the time now, we're still trying to figure out how well we can continue to promote ourselves. Our confidence in our ideas is divided by the sharpness of our pain, our acute frustration with how different life is from what was promised to us. That pain makes us whole, and its examination makes us human. Trying to pretend that we don't feel kills us quicker than death, or at least I think it could.

•

The second Butoh actor did not walk onto the stage; he writhed and crawled, nearly naked under a tattered gray blanket. His movements were grand but subtle. First there was the articulated movement in his steady, heavily knuckled white fingers; his slowly emerging from under the blanket like a nightmare. His movements were less frightening than anticipatory, like how a dream can breed your fear so well you're mesmerized by the character quality of its detail. A careful study. Maybe this is what a master looks like; maybe your dreams know better than anyone else. Perhaps your nightmares are dreams at their highest height; maybe this is what true intimacy looks like.

Intensity is the difference between intimacy and any other type of emotion. The variations between a cuddle and a squeeze can be intimate, but the determination of how close we come is rendered by how far apart we were in the beginning. This means a second part of what renders something intimate is validation. The scary part. We like the kind of validation that affirms us; worships us; tells us we are everything to this world. We need to feel good about our place in the world—rectified, acceptable. But validation is actually the act of checking or proving the accuracy of something, which means it's just as valid for someone who validates you to come back with negative reports as with positive.

I believe true intimacy in all its forms is a balance of this type, of seeing the difference between a cuddle and a squeeze. The intensity: how comfortable we are with the person who is reading us, how comfortable we are with that person coming close, how comfortable we are with the prospect of being read not just in a derogatory way, which we've come to expect, or in a highly lauded way, which we've come to hope for. I imagine both versions are a product of how many of us talk to ourselves based on our childhood and subconscious. *I really am so bad at this. I really am so good at that.* But for someone to honestly read the book of life into us, who does that?

It had been fifteen minutes, and I was still watching the Butoh performer's hand; the bleakness of his skin under the spotlight rendered his gestures two-dimensional. From where I was seated, I could not yet see his face; he had only revealed that part of himself to the people sitting opposite me in the square room stage. The second actor hadn't moved a muscle. I think about the triteness with which I've used that expression before and start to understand what a careful study Butoh must be. I could never master that level of physical control, but I can display that kind of dedication when I see people, see into people, when I listen. The discomfort I felt in the presence of her stillness felt painful, made me restless. Needing a distraction, I wandered off into my loneliest spaces, asking myself if it was harder for people to leave me than stay because my own intimacy is a stillness that reads as control.

A friend of mine, an empath, pointed this out to me once. She is a woman for whom the pain of other people is so real it is hard for her to sit close to you if you are hurting. You don't have to tell her where it hurts or if it hurts for her to feel it. She just does. Her empathic qualities are so resonant that once on a trip to the Nile, a Nubian healer reached out to tell her what a hard time she must have in the world. Of course, for those of us who are skeptics, we might assume that this was the entry point for something he was trying to sell, but he shared nothing else with her other than the opportunity to communicate further should the need arise.

Anyway, on that same Egypt trip the group's confirmed narcissist kept clinging to my friend as if she were feeding off her. It wore her out. It didn't matter to the woman if the validation she presented was positive or negative; it was just the fact that it was, and was constant.

I ask myself now why I'm backing away from talking about the show, and it's because it crossed the threshold inside me that was more intimate, even for me, than I wanted to imagine. The anticipation of seeing the lead actor's face for the first time stirred something chemical in me that lit something I didn't understand. This feeling of sickness, this feeling of being unable to turn away. As if the room were being consumed with a thick fog. I felt hazy. I felt the sharp haze, the sharp click of my body falling asleep with great pain and frustration. I tried to wake myself up because, how embarrassing, in a six-person theater watching the most arresting physical performance that I've ever seen with my body, why would my body be tempted to catnap? But there I was, fighting the urge to drift into my dreamland, to escape.

I consider this a great metaphor for why we culturally have abandoned intimacy for our avatars. What kind of dream we find ourselves seated in isn't just a product of our own narcissism; it is a physical fight within the body to accept that somebody else's reality is a part of our own. Especially if that reality is physically, spiritually, and historically relevant—not the type of story we'd like to tell ourselves about who we are and how we got here, not the type of story we want to read to our inner child at bed.

While watching the Butoh performance I was fighting the memory of one of my inner-child urges: that I used to repeatedly look at books that had pictures of the Hiroshima bombing because I found them fiercely beautiful. It's disgusting to admit that as early as back then, the stark white body parts cast against a black background appealed to me with the drama of art, a theater of the grotesque. I imagine that our teachers showed them to us to try to communicate to us early the depths of human cruelty, to create a generation that was not bound to repeat past mistakes. But there also was the exotic narrativity with which the American history books described the experience, personifying the mushroom cloud as a question mark, white and wide, asking why.

The Butoh performer turned toward me with his mouth open as if he were going to swallow the spirit of the world, slowly unhinging his jaw and turning his body as the music imitated the sound of a low, repetitive human groan. Then, the lights went out, and when they came back on, strobe lights hit each acute movement in the actor's performance as if it were a set of stop-motion photographs. This was validation; the grotesque recognition of what had made this art was not just what Hiroshima had left behind—its imprint—but how Hiroshima opened up ways into how Asian people were being seen as victims.

Think of the photographs that littered my childhood, the advertisements for the Save the Children Fund in which malnourished African and Asian infants who looked almost alien were displayed regularly without any consideration of the cruelty of the gaze, both ours and the camera's. Or the photograph of the napalm girl from the Vietnam War surrounded by screaming children, herself naked, having ripped off her flaming clothes while fleeing a bombing. These photographs appear regularly in my childhood memories as an American, often in stark black and white.

I couldn't bear to watch his face because I didn't want to remember the anguish. I couldn't watch because I didn't want to see the master conjuring the nightmare of our shared history connect it with what lay deep within my subconscious. As much as I believe facing our pain makes us whole, I did not want this closeness to be real. It was too intimate.

The art had clipped back the distance I felt from such horrors in my mind and finally aligned them with my history. As strobe lights flashed across his stark body, I saw flashes of the too-familiar photograph of a whipped slave, the gnarled tree branching across his back so like the blisters blooming, chemical, on the arms of our Japanese brothers. I'd been so blind. It hurts to see each other like this. I almost don't want to. But what can touch us without getting close? I don't know where we are anymore; I don't know what we're supposed to see, or how far we're supposed to love each other. But covering over the places we hurt is not a better decency. Art is how we see our pain. Intimacy is art's fruitage.

That photograph of "Whipped Peter" exposed the brutality of slavery so undeniably that it turned thousands of white people into abolitionists. On his back I see a family tree big enough to track a thousand years and the one billion people who branch from each of us within that time. Intimacy is not about the fact we need each other. It's about facing the fact we are each other. The separations in how we feel are an illusion. The separations in who we are, are a myth. We are each other. And until we're willing to draw close to one another, art is a refuge for me because it helps me see all those places where we overlap.

Leaving the theater a breath of slow air, there had been no real end to the performance. Just the master drawing back from the black like a cloud of smoke and the apprentice returning to consciousness. She woke dreamily and stood beside the door, hugging the corner with the straight of her back just as she had when we entered. The master appeared alongside her—less white, more clothed—welcoming and demure, and beside him, the smiling musician. We bowed deeply to the theater troupe in the narrow exit. We praised them for what never was a performance. On the sidewalk, someone had lit candles and placed a full blooming rose in the tiny cylindrical vase beside each step.

The show was beautiful, but by the time the night ended, I was restless. Back at the hotel, I sat on the edge of the bed scrolling through the day's pictures on my phone when a DM notification floated in from Instagram: "You're in Kyoto? I'm here: . . ." It was Louise. A friend of mine since sixteen whom I hadn't seen since a solo trip to Paris I'd made in 2008. She'd escaped our country hometown on a Fulbright—in the interim, became a burlesque performer—and never looked back. The "here" was a Japanese address with a French name— l'Escamoteur, "the Magician"—not a website or geotag, like a scavenger hunt. I pulled my one going-out outfit from my suitcase.

It is well after midnight when I walk to the hotel door; the doorman asks if he could hail me a taxi. I pause. I ask him for directions to the nearest bus stop; on the walk, I quickly check how to buy tickets. The weather was warm and wet for what I expected in February. A cold-chilled thrill wraps up my nape and around my earlobes at being out alone in the late streets by myself. Just one lonely gentleman in a chef's uniform digging a cigarette into the pavement with his clogs at the bus stop. I practice being Butoh-still, leaning against its railing and later on the bus with my forehead pressed to the glass, staring at the mask of my own reflection. I check my phone to watch my blue dot move closer to my destination. I nearly swoon as I grab the bus railing to exit. Intimacy. All these years of Louise and I knowing each other leading up to this chance moment. This is what makes my heart beat in spite of all the heartache. Life's raw capacity to be sensual and unpredictable.

Louise de Ville and I were grand friends in high school. Her name was different then but the story the same: We had shared the intimate shame of the world being afraid of what we held inside our bodies. The sacral, raw intimacy of us. How close to the world we make men feel when they don't want to, and, for so long, in so many iterations, we had to be punished for that. Our last twilight night on the stage, we were seniors at my high school's open mic doing a cover of "American Woman"—you dancing around in a cheerleading skirt and ski mask, me doing a damn-good deep-throated impression of Lenny Kravtiz. We grooved and sang to each other to the eye drop of everyone. A few years later, Louise went on to become the haute-so-darling of the queer Paris burlesque scene, doing an act in which one morphed from a gorgeous woman to a beautiful man, making the full transformation naked, all while teaching (during the day) on a Fulbright. *We rub each other so close, me in my fishnet stockings. You and I have always had this way to set the world ablaze, even when we hadn't figured out how yet.*

The second floor, cigarette-box-shaped l'Escamoteur is aglow with bordello lamps and smoke-covered cocktails. Frenchmen with string-thin S-curled mustaches called out drinks with names like magic potions. Kyoto after midnight, a second city. Louise and I lean on the bar and run through the highlights of what had been her trip here and what had been for us over a decade. She came to perform at a Tiffany event where she danced in a large martini glass. Airport security hassled her about the rope in her bag—part of the act.

"Oh! For my shibari, sensei," she said, referring to the intimate art of rope bondage, to which she and the two guards gave each other a small bow before they escorted her along. I love her story. It's proof of how comfortably close we can be. How the things we were shamed for in our youth—being too intense, too knowing, too visceral—are becoming what keeps us close to the rest of the world. It's a relief to adventure, to take off the mask and perform as we truly are—formidable. Real intimacy is the only way in this world to truly be brave.

"Quick thinking," I praise, and we clink our glasses to the decades we have spent learning how to use intimacy as a subtle shift in energy. Changing what's secret among us into something respected, we survive our dishonor to become the revered.

On God

Montserrat, Spain

The Black woman is God. That's a phrase I've heard repeatedly, assertively, often. As fact, as camaraderie, as a compliment. As the tagline to a Hotep YouTube PowerPoint presentation filled with exotic drawings of a dark-skinned Mother giving birth to Earth paired with bullet points of questionable science. I find it ironic, to be ordained a deity when it's been a hell of a journey to be treated like a person. To be remembered, respected, or understood. And then I remember, that is very godlike. Being God isn't about being more. It's about being a void that is filled in your absence. Gods don't write the story of who they are, people do, so assured that the truth is derived from their own image.

———

I get a kick out of people who tend to be dogmatic about the things they believe in. About things they believe I should be doing, as if I've never believed in religion. The sanctimony that surrounds yoga, meditation, recycling, getting out in the great outdoors. Hiking. The funny thing about the number of city-dwelling liberals who've tried to get me to hike over the years: they forget I was raised in Kentucky. I can gut a fish and pitch a tent, if I want to. If I want to; I don't.

Hiking, to me, appears to be just as much about elevating walking to sport as it is about elevating it above the walking we do naturally, willingly. It's not about the sweet worship of the bodies we have. It's about waking at an ungodly hour, to catch some errant ray of grace coming over the horizon, at a time when I'm too tired to appreciate it. It's the people who've never had to survive who make fun out of the act of survival.

On the morning of this story, I was still in architecture school at the University of Kentucky. There were about forty of us in First Year, with just shy of a dozen Black and Brown folks. We were whom you might imagine: some Vietnamese college students of varying ages; a Saudi Arabian student who used to carry a prayer rug and bow at least four times a day before 9/11 (then she packed her prayer things away and put an American flag up on her desk); Jill, Jared, and Patrick—the four of us comprising the largest number of African American students the program had ever had at one time. ("Don't worry," the dean told Patrick as he filled out his transfer slip from sociology to architecture, "there's no way all four of you will graduate." It didn't stick, but our fates had already been foreordained.)

Among us was also Vidyuta, whom I'd known since middle school. We'd grown up only a neighborhood apart. Back then, I had marveled at the fluidity with which she passed from one group to another. Indian by heritage but assumed, in that thoughtless Kentucky way, since she wasn't "Black" or "white," to be Mexican. She took it in beautiful stride, over time, befriending a few truly Mexican families, learning the songs they sang when they were celebrating and developing an impressive tolerance for tequila. But that was later. In our middle school years we both went to Lexington Traditional Magnet, where there was a decent influx of Southeast Asian and Middle Eastern students. And she manned the tables of a nervous-looking Brown crew whose parents, like hers, were academics or scientists. But she always stood out, more effervescent, more comfortable than the rest, so it shouldn't have surprised me as much as it did when in our first year of high school she went through another transformation—joining our predominantly white high school's all-white color guard.

Between middle and high, she started dating a tall trombone player, the boy-next-door who'd been courting her all summer.

When he stopped being her boyfriend, I started to hear tales of her sights set on a star football player, the girl from my middle school becoming a presence around the varsity lunch tables—the cafeteria, the segregated epicenter of American high school gossip, a land less faithful than Judas Iscariot.

"Vid-yu-ta?" I said when I saw her, unintentionally correcting the pronunciation of her first name, which had morphed more into "Va-judah" amid her new, cool friends. I'd seen so many iterations of the girl-at-a-distance by the time we got to college together I wasn't sure which one was the best to approach. But that was the beauty of Vidyuta. No matter where she was on campus or at cafeteria tables, the arrow of her heart, her integrity, always pointed up. A north brilliant and real. Someone who never had a bad word to say about anyone but always knew what was what. It's surprising we didn't become friends sooner. But, as she puts it, she was always scared of me for the same reason I was scared of her—I assumed she was cool and unfriendly, and that was that. We became friends over a monk buffet on the top of Montserrat—but I'm getting ahead of myself; I have to go back to the point where the five of us who make this story found each other in architecture. The moment we shared, witnessing the Black Virgin, on a pilgrimage none of us asked for.

•

The First Years are standing in an old square in Barcelona, a two-week spring break study abroad trip. Seventy students and four professors. Once we gather, one of the professors tells us he's booked a day trip for all of us out of town that will begin at five a.m., a hike.

"Tomorrow morning, we're going to climb Montserrat," he says, flipping the gold carabiner on his portable water bottle. He stands six foot four, redheaded, in mountain boots and Carhartt trousers. The rest of us are finally beginning to pass diplomatically among the more streamlined Europeans, in trench coats and low-profile sneakers. We'd grown used to this kind of thing from him, because this was exactly the type of curveball he'd throw anytime we grew comfortable—either to make us cultured or because he was masochistic. At the beginning of the week, he'd told us all to just throw out our maps of the city.

"Just draw your way through it," he said. Several of the students got almost irretrievably lost, but the professor never suffered the consequences of his expectations; he just continually insinuated we weren't committed enough. We tried to adhere. We wanted to believe in the dogma of becoming great architects. But, a week later, when all the professors contracted food poisoning eating at local restaurants he'd selected from what he claimed were authentic leads, we students started eating at the Hard Rock Cafe three times a day and stopped adhering to his church of learning as doctrine. That's one of the things I've come to know about divine order. It sneaks up on you. We stood in an old square in the Barri Gòtic, making no protests about our trip to a monastery the next morning, beginning with the five a.m. train.

The Montserrat monastery is a bit of an architectural marvel. A place of communion carved in the side of a mountain by Benedictine monks. At least three of our four professors of architecture were Catholics of some sort—our leader the most devoted—and, at home, we lived in the South. It was almost impossible to participate in the culture without claiming allegiance to one divine ordinance or another; put that on God.

The thing that bothered me most about the way that God operated for college students is that professors often reduced the content of our faith, in deference to some universal knowledge, a greater academic truth. For our professor, that truth was a faith in a puritanical, maniacal work ethic. "I don't believe in creativity, I only believe in work," he'd tell us. In his studio, he believed in long hours and little sleep, as a sign of productivity, a formula that turned even the most zealous of his followers insane. Some of the students would even jokingly refer to him as "God." The dictator of all their decisions.

"Hm," he said, overhearing the nickname in studio one day. He liked it.

God helps those who help themselves. There was a simple

Darwinism in the professor's approach to who should become an architect. A pseudoscience. A belief system he cultivated all his own, based on books he was knowledgeable about, Eastern philosophy he was not, and a severe slant of prejudice. This for me is why I can no longer call myself a Christian. I've been tethered to and exhausted by it too many times, by a white man trying to craft himself in God's image. I've given up on worshipping anyone who can't imagine a world with me in it. Most of the time, "God" is a man of big insecurities and very little faith, casting down judgment from a pulpit in which he positions himself as the Creator. An architect or the Architect, it makes no difference. We followed "God" less because we were believers and more because our attendance in his class affected our grade, and so we stumbled sleepily to the Eurail at the crack of dawn, snoozing as the train tucked into the prayer rhythm of its tracks for as long as possible. But still, we followed him, and in the end, I knew he wasn't Him.

I'm no prophet, but I predicted that a punctual appearance at the base of the rock wasn't going to be enough to satisfy "God's" class requirements. He had something else up his sleeve; he always did.

"The best way to make it up the mountain at sunrise is if we climb it," he said, stretching out his large hand like megachurch Jesus. Not a hike. A veritable mountain climb. Much of the student-flock began to timidly follow, but I decided to stick close to the other teachers, who seemed to be whispering dissent among themselves. Hypocrisy, just what I needed. Glory, they had plotted for themselves an alternate route. Those of us who were skeptical about "God's" cult instead followed their lead.

As the saying goes, "If the mountain won't come to Muhammad," take the ski lift. The ski lift trek was led by Melody, my favorite of all the First Year profs. She had the most ingenious hand-eye coordination I had ever seen, could sketch nearly everything, from a cracked skull to a rusted muffler, in exquisite detail and proportion, like the Renaissance designer using a free-hand sketch of a perfect circle as his only artistic résumé. The only professor in our program who was open about her devout religious faith, Melody was excited to reach the summit.

"You know," she said as the ski lift landed the last of us down, in under six minutes, among what might as well have been the clouds of heaven, "this monastery is the site of one of the world's few remaining Black Virgins." Her enthusiasm was pure, none of the "you're welcome for trying to educate you about your own Blackness" that often accompanied any mention of heritage for Black kids in school.

"You know that Montserrat is home to one of the only remaining Black Madonnas in southern Europe," said a second professor, to me, in the tradition of the latter. It had been a few hours and I was sitting in a corner, watercoloring a painting I'd made of a massive rock formation above the monastery walls, a respite from the rest of the mountain, which looked, by comparison, imposing. I ignored him, and walked toward the edge of the cliff where the mountain's trail ended. A few pebbles skipped beneath my tennis shoes, down into the chasm thousands of feet below, where the abbey started. I was trying to see if any of "God's" apostles had made it close to the monastery yet. No one. I spent another hour combing the aisles of the abbey gift shop, turning over postcards and bottles of mead.

I didn't want to see a Black Madonna. I was still a practicing Christian up to that point, and somehow, the presence of a black woman depicted as the mother of God was anathema to what I knew as truth. Blasphemous. Wasn't done. I wasn't on that "Jesus is white" shit. But I took the "Jesus is Black" kick as a stretch. The Jesus I knew was Jewish. Semitic. Some version of west Asian and Middle Eastern I knew was not me. I saw this as a more enlightened version of the "Black" versus "white" argument. Despite the church infrastructure, the Christian faith and faithful have always been multicultural, international so to speak. But I didn't know this back then, and so finding a Black Madonna in Spain frightened me because I couldn't imagine how she got there.

The church that I grew up in didn't listen to gospel music. It was deeply reformist and had developed its own hymns, so it wasn't until I was far out of college that I first listened to Aretha Franklin's live album *Amazing Grace*, recorded in

New Temple Missionary Baptist Church, and considered our evangelical power. "Amazing Grace" was a song I knew well, simply because in a high school dance class, when I had refused to perform to it (not wanting to participate in what my parents deemed "false religion"), the choreographer explained to me a story shared with her about the lyrics. They didn't come from the church; they came from the Middle Passage. A young woman being deported from her homeland, to be sex trafficked and forced into brutal labor, saw that a sailor on the ship was dying and offered him her food. It saved him. He never saw that girl again. But the humanity, the divinity, she showed despite her fate moved the sailor to write a song.

Aretha Franklin sings "Amazing Grace," purged clear and opalescent. The hymn is a dialogue between herself and a higher power, but she's the only one who speaks. Sometimes, it's hard for me to attribute the gifts of Black women to a higher power because I have seen us spend so much time in this world devoid of grace outside what we bring to the altar ourselves. Grace is what we're asked to display whenever the burden is too heavy. Aretha Franklin sings "Amazing Grace" trembling, trying not to tumble. But only her own voice moves the rock out the way of her salvation. Why is that?

Say grace. The grace of God is what we are told to give rather than receive. And yet, when I think of all Aretha Franklin survived, I have to ask, what wretched thing had she ever needed to atone for? That voice. That gift. That body. That spirit surviving years of abuse. "And grace will lead you home," she sings, and I think of the girl who gave the wretched her food, and see home in the way she must have looked at him. I am still trying to get there. Asking why God why God why have you forsaken us?

I had rounded the carousel of monastery greeting cards one more time, reading and putting things back. A third request to visit the Holy Virgin came to me, this time from a friend.

"Sis, you gonna go see the Black Madonna?" asked Jared. Later in our adulthood, Jared and I would spend a decade trading scriptures between each other, and updating each other on what versions of the Bible were our favorites, before giving Christianity up—our world's too filled with cruelty and uncertainty. Those exchanges would be beautiful though and, likely, began right there in a Benedictine monastery where I saw the presence of a black deity as a threat to my spirituality where Jared saw affirmation.

"Doesn't it feel a bit . . . you know—?" I said.

"I know," said Jill. She had walked up among us and stood beside me in the middle of our conversation. I didn't have to explain to Jill, a Black Christian woman, how I felt. She knew the word I was searching for was "sacrilegious." She had just arrived at the monastery, a member of "God's" crew who had finally ascended the mountaintop, her face flushed and her gait stiff. (I didn't know it then but Jill was the first person I encountered with Ehlers-Danlos syndrome; I had no idea how much she suffered.)

The rest of the architecture students were stumbling in, dappled in the mud of atonement. It was now or never. Pretty soon the room would be too crowded with dewy academia to take in the sanctified marvel of one of the world's last remaining Black Women—the Madonna—an icon.

•

"Eli eli lama sabachthani." Instead of a prayer, the words I uttered in front of the Holy Black Virgin were Jesus' last. There I was, and it was hard to look at her. Because I was so unaccustomed to gazing upon an artifact of religion's glory and seeing my face? How did I worship, blind to myself, for so many years? How did I get here? How did she?

"Goodness," said Patrick, gazing upon her gilded beauty. "Maybe she's here because of the Moors." The fact the Spaniards were Moorish would suggest the use of a brown-skinned version would have been a better conversion tactic for their people than a pale white woman. This was graceful. Jared kept checking in on Jill and me, affirming Patrick's explanation. He hoped that us too-good Black girls would feel better about seeing ourselves as the bosom of God if we could give it a secular context.

———

About fifteen years later, someone I met had a curious friend who had visited a Satanist temple. According to him, the friend reported back to everyone he knew that an Eve, the Seat of Creation, who was definitively a Black woman, was at the center of Satanist ideology. In the center of a church was a larger-than-life Black icon who carried not a rock on her back, but a baby in her belly. I've never done the research. "Church of Satan" is not a rabbit hole I want in my browser history. But even though by the time I heard this I'd put Christianity aside, I shivered at the thought that Satanists did a better job of representing the historical Cradle of the Earth than Christianity.

"Sounds like the Church of Satan could use a rebrand," I joked. But the thought lingered. And I thought to myself, what's it even mean to have a Church of Satan? Was it once the Church of Lucifer? Had the Scriptures misinterpreted? "The shining one" of Isaiah 14:12 representing not the Devil, but a King of Light?

That's the trouble with God. Everyone I know means "God" differently, and not a single one of us can prove the other is not right. The concept of worship is confusing. Long after I'd left behind a church, but not God, I was joking with a Mexican friend of mine about seeing the Black Madonna, expecting him to find the story unusual. An ex-Catholic, he was awed because, according to him, in Central America the viewing of a Black Madonna is a rare and special privilege. According to him, it was Black women who first brought Christianity to Europe and beyond. And despite all the years I had spent studying the Bible, it had never occurred to me that, geographically, that was the only thing that made sense.

It took confirmation by my first Kundalini guru—of all people—for me to accept this. She, a diversely Black woman in Brooklyn. We were practicing one day when, apropos of nothing, she said she felt compelled to tell me a story. And the urge was right. She mentioned she'd been reading that the presence of Black Madonnas on multiple continents is because Ethiopian Coptic Christians had been among the earliest missionaries. Just think of it: Jesus in Palestine. His apostles spreading the word all through the world by foot. Naturally, the migration of the Way, the Truth, and the Light was cradled in Northern Africa and moved upward. Some of the oldest Christian churches still exist there.

And knowing what the Black women of this world have done with the Word through gospel, it only makes sense that some of the first disciples in whom the Fruit of Christ set bloom thousands of years ago were some of their sisters. Then as now, our tongues were lit with the fire of the Good Word and our sandals never seemed to retire from the work of preaching. In that zeal, it is easy to imagine black women among the first flock who traveled through Turkey, and Portugal, until they reached the Spaniards, sharing along the way not only the gospel but—according to what amused my Kundalini instructor—new crops, herbs to grow as medicine, and the knowledge of how to use them. Because, on the road to saving the world, they knew there would be times when they needed to save themselves.

My guru explained that often the black women who took these pilgrimages later became canonized as saints because they were healers. I couldn't believe this. But I could believe this. Because when Jesus said, "Wash your hands and become clean in the blood of the Lamb," black women would have taken that seriously, cleansing Europeans of the disease and pestilence that plagued them.

I've seen nothing more lamblike than the woman whose face I peered into at Montserrat, the Black Madonna.

"There's a tear in her eye," I cried, worrying time might be ruining her with condensation.

"It's a miracle," Patrick said. "That's what they call it."

Consider a brown-skinned God. Think of black people as Christ's earliest disciples. I need this salvation of history because it means, as Black and Brown folk today, we were not just the brutally converted and colonized Christians, but the original ones. When I struggle to understand the way we cling to the Christian faith despite all it has done to tell us we are not worthy, it makes sense to me that we do this with the deep love of those who had already heard the Word of God before the Bible was even completed. The Messiah was ours. We spread his message. Which is why he took root in our hearts the way he did. Our religion was never first a white man's book. Which is why Aretha Franklin sings grace so close to the grain and why grace knew that God would not forsake her on either side of the Pacific Ocean.

●

When "God" finally emerged from his sweaty pilgrimage, he looked revived, but the slowest of his disciples were badly scratched and dehydrated. There was a crazed reverie in his eyes; he was still spouting his useless propaganda.

"You know, after such a vigorous workout it's best to consume only water," he explained. To baptize the pain with more pain. To fast and give yourself enough time for the toxins to flush out your body. Tight-lipped, Vidyuta took one look at him and headed straight to the Benedictine buffet, piling her plate high with meat and mashed potatoes. The Black woman is God. Her love of what was good for her body, her resistance, was spiritual to me. God made man in his image, and yet a man as "God" has failed me so consistently. But the God in the womb—its emptiness and honesty—that is a god I can real-deal with. In Vidyuta, I saw the truth of the transmutable woman and I began to love her, unquestionably, forever. When I tell her, years later, how much this moment inspired me, she laughs.

"I was just hungry," she says. Who of us isn't? It's simple. Every day I see God in the truths that set us free.

On Dying

Maastricht, Netherlands

Oma's body turned blue and gray long before her last day on earth. Her fingers were always stained with newsprint, pur-plish, a Rorschach blot of the world's collected sorrows. She would sit and digest the paper diligently, scanning the world news from across the globe. She was never without some know-ing antidote—or I should say anecdote—about contempo-rary culture's troubles, which she would share with me in a Dutch I mostly didn't understand.

She spoke slowly for me, with gravity and meaning. We didn't know each other well, but I loved her. Much before we met, before she became my grandmother-in-law, she asked the family to start bringing her newspapers with more infor-mation on current events in America so that she would have plenty of things to ask me. To be knowledgeable of despite our limitations in Dutch and English. I admired her for this refusal to see language as a barrier as long as the information shared between us was factual; I still get a lot out of this thought. Sometimes, at my most gezond (meaning "healthy"), I want to peel back the layers in human culture and just speak truth into it, the raw burden of bones and cartilage. I see this in my memory of how Oma lived.

She sits at the end of one of our Sunday visits dredging coins from her purse. She pulls from her coin purse enough hard change for a broodje gezond, "healthy sandwich"— which is how I learn the word and the phrase. We were to go to the local deli and request for ourselves the same sandwich she and her husband had shared for years, splitting it between our fingers, an act of love.

When Oma's blue was no longer just newsprint, I started to worry. She'd always been stoic, not the kind of plump, rosy creature one might imagine attaching the word "grandmother" to. But Oma was a powerful listener. Her face would come alive as she sat alert in an easy chair, especially on the day when—to celebrate our being together—she had ordered vlaai from a fancy bakery, of the utmost quality, with fresh strawberries and cream. She watched us eat the dessert but took little for herself. She stayed as watchful as a soldier as we sliced the pie for more.

"Enjoy," she said, one English word. Enjoy.

•

I was learning about war; what it meant for the people of the Netherlands to have been survivors of the largest and deadliest war in history. There are ways that the trauma showed up in both the young and old that I couldn't have imagined back in America. For instance, my husband and I had developed a close friendship with a couple in their eighties. Joan and Harry Driessen. A couple who had the most romantic meet-cute in Dublin. An entirely fairy-tale beginning. Harry had been a sailor in the merchant marine, soon after World War II ended. She was an Irish ballerina convalescing from tuberculosis in the home of her elderly grandparents—an orphan. It was Christmas Eve. When he saw her through the frost of a window eating supper with her grandparents, she was the most beautiful woman he'd ever seen. His friend, a fellow sailor, knocked on the door. They bid the family a good Christmas, the family let them in, and years later, despite all the bumps and scrapes of human-being, here they were, still here.

Harry delighted over little things, like kappertjes, "capers," or the simplicity of canned tomatoes, fresh and red. After living through both world wars, he still carried the memory of scarcity in his body, like a bird that had roosted and nested there. He would tell us stories about times when he was so hungry as a boy during the First that he would run in the direction of gunshots—instead of away from them—knowing that somewhere he might find empty trenches that still carried supplies. He never mentioned the dead men he surely found there.

The war showed up in other ways, even in the generation half the Driessens' age. Women like Marricka, the person I often accompanied when volunteering at the Dutch refugee camp. She had strict rules about where hot water came from and how you used it. One day, because it was cold and we were headed out to work, I turned the tap in my kitchen to fill my water bottle, hot, so that I would have not only the warmth of the water to drink but also the heat of the bottle to hold in my hands . . .

"You can't drink hot water from the sink!" Marricka said. "It has to be boiled!!" I looked at her quizzically. The water that came from the faucet was nearly scalding. She started to consider the thing she said. Where did it come from?

"Oof, the war . . . ," she said, as if it were some kind of explanation in itself. She was in her midforties. It wasn't about memory, since she hadn't lived it; it was about the legacy of families like hers.

When it came to the trauma of being torn apart by soldiers and social hierarchies—maybe this is why Oma read the news. Maybe this is why she poured her spirit into the newspapers so diligently. She looked to establish a sense of normalcy, to not be caught off guard, looking into the core of people, the code, the very fabric of our existence. She wanted to see how our DNA rippled and eddied, and what might take shape. She did not want another global conflict to catch her unawares and dislodge the bedrock of her life in what was still—despite the new century—a postwar era. A postwar era is never so. How often I forget the trauma and tragedy that has beset so many people I've loved from Palestine, Syria, Sudan, Rwanda. The era goes on. There is no "post" dying.

Oma was moving out of her body long before she had told us she'd decided she would no longer live in her body. She had decided on assisted suicide. She had picked a date, chosen an end-of-life plan, and it was a hard thing to hear but the logic was clear. It had been a month or two since our last visit and Oma arrived at the door pushing a walker, something she'd never done. Ashamed as I am I thought this way, I was a bit annoyed that everything took her so much longer, her movements so cautious and deliberate. I missed the strong woman with the sharp mind. I realized part of the reason we had waited so long since our last visit was because we couldn't stand watching her age so fast; we were in denial about it. Oma saw everything. She had made a plan to do something about it.

Of course we protested, as if we were going to actually do something to change the direction of our lives so that it better accommodated her increasing frailty. But, in reality, we are selfish in the way starting a new family condones, out with the old, and none of that really helped Oma. She struggled to escort us to the lobby of the nursing home, to see us out to the car and get a bit of sun, as she always did. One chink in the concrete and she almost tumbled onto the uneven pavement. It was frightening. We would say, "Poor Oma," in the car but not much else, my husband and I wrapping up our grief like a crumpled newspaper.

"Oma walked through two world wars," the family would sometimes say proudly as a sign of her imperturbable immortality. Somehow, despite her age, we took her as someone we never needed to worry about, but that was our naïveté. We were underestimating what survival had cost her, the price of what she had seen: so many deaths, so much tragedy. And now, nearly ninety, she described with an open despair that nearly everyone she'd befriended upon entering the nursing home had now died, and she was differently alone than she had been in decades before. Even when her children visited frequently, it was never as often as before, Oma crossing off each of the days on the calendar she kept hung on the wall across from her stack of newspapers and easy chair.

The only person who was always there was Sara—her daughter, in her midsixties and described by Oma as "special needs." She lived one building over in a similarly constructed assisted living facility. Sara would come and sit across from her mother as part of her daily routine. They chatted, or silently did the crossword in the company of one another. That was real love too.

Much of what motivated Oma to pick a death date was that she had weighed the frequency of Sara's visits against the rarity of those of her sons and their children, and had said to herself she didn't want to be the kind of mother who disappeared. It would be easier for Sara—who could grasp many things, but for whom time was still a constant struggle—if she knew when her mother would be dying. It was another gift she could give to her child, a few last days of certainty.

Sara and Oma rehearsed the date for months. It was circled in red on her wall calendar, and each day she and Sara would sit across from it and run through exactly what would happen on the days to follow. She would run drills:

"Sara, where will you go on the days that follow when I'm not here anymore? Who will you go see in the months and weeks to fill the void of time that we so often spend together?" Sara committed each detail to her memory, the names of the friends she was meant to visit on those future days when her mother was no longer available to be a friend to her. Sara repeated the information as matter-of-fact. No longer a tragedy, an ending, just a simple assessment of the truth. Like a newspaper. One day, her mother wouldn't be there anymore, and then she'd sit across from new people, quietly doing the crossword. Some of the people included in Sara's strategic plan,

Oma had never met. But she listened to Sara's stories—read, projected, surmised.

I still admire this greatly about Oma. We underestimate the strength of a woman who can read the world well, even when nestled in it at one small vantage point. It is a skill I hope to cultivate in this life, if I am not too selfish.

On a visit a few weeks before her death date, Oma and Sara patiently walked through the post-death plans for us in the most matter-of-fact tone possible. *Oh, my God*, I thought to myself, *the Dutch are just too crazy*. I rubbed my forehead, held my breath; it agitated me to think how everybody in the family was talking about dying as if this weren't the end of a loved one. I couldn't stand it. I sat with my mouth gaping wide as Sara explained her days after her mother was gone—the next day, and the next—as if the grief of losing her mother wasn't even a consideration. It all seemed too cynical. Dying for me always had to be accompanied by the chaotic abyss of losing someone and the darkness that consumed you. Humbling yourself to losing, until it had stolen so much of you that everyone was worried about you by the time you decided to return to earth. I hate that, when I actually analyze the ways that I've been taught to process grief; I understand this too is unhealthy. I blamed Sara's lack of emotion on what the family described as her "low intellect." This didn't feel right either. What I had been taught about loss is that it must destroy you in order for it to have validity. What I have been taught about death is that it must surprise you in order for us to grieve it.

Oma taught me that dying is just a way. There was beauty in knowing. And Sara, courageous Sara, approached her mother's decision with respect for her sacrifice. Less time on earth, more certainty together. Something that death in its natural state would have taken away. It would take me decades before I digested Oma's choice as what it really was, love beyond my own comprehension.

In Oma's final days, she was happy. She got to meet her first great-grandchild, a miracle. Her living living on. This was exactly the kind of end she wanted, a polite entrance, not a grand exit. She had dreams of the kind of death that didn't stop and break us down completely. But the day of death was difficult.

Oma had picked out her death-day outfit and propped herself up on the bed in an array of clean sheets and cross-stitched pillows, ready to recite a few words she had written for each of us, and prepared to leave us each a token to remember her by. Oma, the woman whom I'd known to be pristinely organized, had signed all the documents for assisted suicide, "in sound body and sound mind," carefully covering all the legalities with my father-in-law, her eldest son. All of us were clear about the details. She would be administered a slowly increasing morphine drip until she drifted off to the place beyond headlines. But the journey wasn't as easy as it had been in the fine print.

Let's just say none of it happened the way she planned it. Aside from the hospital staff, none of us could have prepared for the fact that Oma was allergic to morphine. The woman who walked through two world wars. Who'd never needed opioids. The IV burned through her veins. Her frail arms itched so bad, they blistered, then bled. She was begging the hospital staff for something to take the edge off dying this way, but the documents were clear: her life would end that day, that way, by contract. The once-supportive hospital staff turned clinical and antagonistic. It was in the fine print. If she couldn't stand the morphine, she would die by dehydration.

"Not like this," I said, "not like this." The truth upset us all, but we trudged on. Oma's final war was to be with the system. My mother-in-law held a bedpan by her mouth while Oma vomited in between reading index cards. Her voice was raspy and weakening.

"Ze-lah," she sputtered, "Ze-lah!" She had gotten to me, the room's sixth family member. I loved the way she said my name, the "Z"; I never corrected her. In her hand was a sapphire necklace with a tiny fleck of diamond; I expected nothing other than the chance to get to say goodbye. I couldn't help but cry. It wasn't what we were supposed to do. Then just as I held her hand and muttered, "Thank you," she began vomiting so profusely the medical team was called in. We were all ushered out of the room as a family. I never saw her again.

We waited in the nursing home waiting room for a few hours before my father- and mother-in-law returned, white as paper.

"Oh, my son," my father-in-law said. "It just doesn't seem like this should be the only way to do this." It was the first time I understood the grief they covered over wasn't crazy, just different. He was right. It just seemed for a woman of this much integrity, this kind of suffering was not owed. But when do we ever dictate the violence of our own circumstances? Harry Driessen as a boy, joyously running toward the bullets firing over farmland, knowing that at their end he would find food.

I believe not growing up with that same sense of war gives Americans a disadvantage on dying. Worldwide, we cause chaos, but we don't partake of it ourselves. We view death as something unnatural and yet somewhere, we are bombing mothers and children. And yet, as an American, I questioned whether one old woman determining her death was right. We treat death as unnatural in America because we believe we hold power over it, when in reality, it is as constant as laughter, and love, and reading the newspaper, and—every now and then—an old woman folds her periodical across her lap and decides today is her last day to read it.

I began to understand Oma's stance on dying when I attended her funeral. She was not religious. She picked a nondenominational meeting space provided by her assisted living facility with a few rows of chairs surrounded by stained glass. The pulpit was there, the organ open, but no one went up to play or speak. She wanted it that way. On the lectern, she'd provided printouts of her favorite poems. We read them quietly, some out loud, a means of communication. In the background, the facility played a soundtrack she'd curated. The service was elegant. Specific. I learned that afternoon that Oma's two sons had been estranged for years and she worried about, in grief, their interacting. She tried to provide them a blank canvas, the truth of their communion. Oma alive, in death. As we were leaving the chapel my father-in-law turned to his brother and hugged him. It was the first time my mother-in-law cried that day. They hadn't embraced since before my husband was born.

Less than a year after Oma's dying, my husband and I moved to Bloomington, Indiana. In the Midwest, I heard the phrase "letting the barn die," in reference to the farmers who, instead of deconstructing a building that was no longer in use, would let it dilapidate naturally. In the letting, there was beauty. The letting, as the barn, once black, turned blue and silver hues. As the roof and beams turned over their age in sunlight. And there was the way the barn leaned just more than it should in the wind—tenuous, ready for its final deployment.

On Dancer

Bloomington, Indiana

PART I

2013. I asked him when we first met if his name was Rooster or Sammy Davis Jr. Jr., and his ears perked up at the latter, like the promise of something he'd become. Everybody needs someone who sees in them the divine when they are struggling to make it out of their lowest point. He was dirty. He had given up on life. He was so sick, the entire staff at the kill shelter believed he couldn't be rehabilitated. Then he was mine.

Sammy Davis Jr. Jr. was the auspicious name of the official seeing eye dog in the book I loved. *Everything Is Illuminated.* With the character of the dog's owner, I shared a love of the debonair and undeniable elegance of Sammy Davis Jr. Sr. The primogenitor, the beauty.

When Sammy dances, I see his namesake, namely, a photograph where his obsidian skin lights in front of a silk Cadillac and a gauzy Marilyn Monroe. He glitters with his legs akimbo and I forget that he was anything to the world other than a dancer. And I forget I've loved anyone more than I've loved my dog. That's not true. What I really see is how much my dog loves me. The way his elegant body slid under the tarp we'd tethered to the car, trying to make sure he didn't pee all over a recently leased vehicle, which he did anyway, scurrying, his tail in circles as we tried to retrieve him from where he burrowed beneath the back of the driver's-side seat. I loved him, because I know what it's like to struggle that much to survive. Know what it takes to keep a fight alive in you. Know what it takes to keep a fight alive in your bones, till it is rhythmic, and certain, and undeniably happy.

People often ask me if my dog has a glass eye—as Sammy did. No. But at his age, he surrendered his eyesight to cataracts, which makes his dance indefatigable, special, unique. The tiny thing parading at the front door on two legs each time I make an entrance, as if each reentrance is fabulous. I think, *How incredible*, remembering the original, the father, and how much we've never celebrated him as a half-blind dancer, a hero, a pirouetting cyclops who couldn't have known where he would land—or did he—which was in history. I mean, he never let his disability define who he was. It just refined him. I hope to become more like him every day. I'm thinking of the two of them tap-dancing at top speed—and the dog and the dancer only remind me of the ways I've been immune to myself.

Abused myself. There was a time when I wasn't going to let my dog love me. I was convinced that if I couldn't make love work in the form of a person, I didn't deserve it. I was so convinced that if I couldn't make my husband love me, I wasn't worth it. I danced around the kitchen in bare feet, in an apron, canning things. It was a performance. Which Sammy Davis Jr.'s dancing never is. You can tell because his work was paid but never transactional. "I've got to be me," he said. And even though it was the standard, he meant it—the dog and the man; I, on the other hand, was still "you're nobody till somebody loves you," a song Sammy covered with panache and irony, the dance of love requiring a little more self-awareness than I had back then. Me, sitting in an empty rental-apartment kitchen. Hoping the jeweled jars I made of a neighbor's tomatoes were enough reason to stick around; the eloquent beauty I can make when gifted absolutely nothing but a little bit of patience and respect.

He didn't come home for hours. For what felt like days often—the husband, not the dog—and I grew sick in the decision that I was truly nobody to love, since my husband was already leaving me, long before we divorced. But up out of my lamenting, there was the dog: the debutante, the debonair, softly crooning me into submission with his half-blind puppy-dog eyes. As if he were holding an old-school microphone to his snout; in his black fur and white feet, a coat-and-tails tuxedo. "You're somebody," he said, "I'm somebody who loves you." I know it was just a sly trick he played back in his puppyhood to get me to let him put his paws on the leather sofa—where he was forbidden, the leather sofa we could barely afford.

●

I knew when my husband bought me the dog that he was leaving me; its dance would be a slow and painful process. He was meant to break me down and then build me up like architecture. I described this process to a friend of mine, talking about how they built the High Line in New York City. I was an architect working in the Fashion District. They were "letting the barn die," the railroad in the middle of the city.

"You see, you let things weather past the point of return so that you can build them back up in whatever way you shape them."

"That's a beautiful concept," they said, "that's a great brand. Is there a word for that? What would you call it?"

"That's colonialism," I said to them, and they laughed. "The word is 'America.'"

"You right," they said, "you right."

I'm talking about New York because I used to lie under the Manhattan Bridge overpass with my Dutch then-fiancé when

Brooklyn Bridge Park was just a berm of overgrowth along the Hudson. And the young woman refurbishing the carousel would sit for hours in the sun getting people to sign the petition to encase it in glass, in a more permanent structure. We knew that part of the city like the backs of our hands. We held the backs of each other's hands and took care of each other, we got married there, moved to the Netherlands for a brief spell. In the end, it was too racist, under the spell of its own Trumpian architect, the archetype—Geert Wilders, Dutch leader of the Freedom Party, who, soon after I arrived in the Netherlands, flew to New York as the special guest star of an anti-Muslim protest in which participants desecrated Korans. So we moved away.

The problem with being the architect of somebody else's desire is that the impulse itself is a careful dance between the partner and the creator. Some people use the dance to bend the will of a nation. Some people use the dance to give birth to a new age. I knew earlier than I'd probably ever admit that I would dedicate my womb to the world, the word. If you believe my husband did not know this, you believe he was a stupid man.

He's not. He made me believe that I brought the dog home. He had been out trying to find himself, gallivanting about town. Finding a new childhood. Tearing down the very fabric of my architecture. When he brought me the dog, the Dancer,

I named him Sammy Davis Jr. Jr. because in his eyes I saw the archetype of a man who would never break me.

He taught me things, he loved me things, he loved me beloved; I wore an apron for him—the man—I tried everything I could, as I got better, I learned more words for "better," he couldn't understand, my English. I tried to be a good housewife.

I fell sick. He was gone to do God knows what. He told me the dog would take care of me.

He was gone.

Every time I'd come home the Dancer would greet me like he'd missed me, hard. It would be hard. The man came back. I would lie in bed with my soon-to-be ex, and the dog would sometimes steal my glasses or earbuds and chew on them nervously in the night waiting for me to come find him. The dog slept between us. The dog, the baby, the Dancer, and the dog crept closer to my side, as the wedge between the man and me grew deeper.

By the time he watched my husband punch the wall by my head to keep me from going out, the Dancer would never let him back near the bed again. We don't reconcile. But the man, now with nowhere to go, sleeps across the hall and the dog lies prone on the end of the king-size bed beneath me, a sentry.

I was having nightmares, violent nightmares that said, *get out get out get out!* and I just didn't have enough money yet. To keep me, he put us in deeper debt. By the time he finally left the country—and me—for good, I was working under the table at a local grocery just to pay him back. The Man—the Credit Union—the man was gone.

I had violent nightmares about the last fight we had, where I told him:

"I don't want to feel like your mother anymore," as we stood at the threshold to our home.

"Aww, twelve years a slave . . . ," he replies, and I slap him, hard, the black dog barking back, *on dancer, on dancer, on dancer!*

I tell him, "I don't want to be your wife anymore. Because you are too stupid." And we get in the car and drive to the Chase Bank to get in front of a notary and sign the divorce papers. It was not a happy day. It would be another six months to a year (what was it? What was it before I was free of him?), and the dog kept fighting for me, going into the guest room even after the man had flown off—every now and then—to shit on the carpet.

I take the Dancer to the vet. I thought there was something wrong with him. The vet asks me, "Is there someone in the house he is mad at?" I laugh. I tell him that someone had just left.

The first new person I made love to in the king-size bed was skinny enough to fit into my yoga pants. The crack of his ass tasted like lemon rinds. He wore my clothes home after the dog peed all over his.

"He is no good for you," the dog said, and thank God that the dog was the deity backward when lovers felt farther away than clouds.

The dog took care of me. The dog poured into me like no spirit had before. I say, *on, dancer* because he is an ancient being who crossed light-years to save me. A rescued traveler who crossed worlds.

I took him to the park, where he would eat the persimmons that fell to the ground until his shit turned gold; he was so happy. He ran down the hill with so much speed, his body spun in the air in a full 360 and we looked at each other:

"Did you see that?"

"Would you look at that?!"

PART II

I divorced my husband before he could divorce me of myself. Everyone wants to break the breakable girl inside the unbreakable Black woman. I wasn't going to let it happen. Drag saved me. Almost every night, in the wake of my divorce, I would hit up one of the queer clubs on Bloomington's outskirts or downtown—Uncle E's, the Back Door. The Root Cellar wasn't gay but it smelled like it, down to the $2 pickleback shots, and we would cycle back and forth between one's disco heat and the other's underground barn funk. I wasn't ready to come out yet. But I was willing to find myself and become a regular.

Uncle E's lost its liquor license. A common problem in Bloomington, a town of the underprivileged, the highly educated, and the overtly creative. A means of thought control.

I arranged my weekends around supporting events at the Back Door, like sex shows where pale men slit their tongues and bled on baby dolls, tied their Barbie-doll partners up in shibari ropes for a $5 cover. But, in the beginning, there was drag. There was always drag. And the drag was fabulous.

A little-known secret about middle-American drag: it's the glitteriest because our mothers are the prettiest. Those southern Midwestern mothers—trapped baby dolls—modeling what you can do with very little money and very few shopping options, sequins and rhinestones to buff like gems. They taught us good-quality fabric, high hair, and hotter poses. Perfect matte lipstick that emphasizes the rim, not the lip.

High hair and hotter poses. I don't remember the names of any of the girls who used to perform those nights, but I remember the images they were each playing to their mothers. A big-bodied blonde who bartended every night that wasn't drag night showed me pictures of his Colombian mother. She'd married his father, from South Bend, out of something that sounded like an arrangement. She cried every night. He extended the waistline of her quinceañera dress and wore it down the runway of the Back Door like a pageant queen. Her golden performance. She sang "I'm Every Woman."

I've met cis women opposed to the idea of drag. I could have been one of them. Until I started to understand the stories: the highest odes to femininity. It's not a critique of where women fall short. It is the boys who have watched the girls be bullied, letting free the girl inside themselves and taking her out of her unbreakable cellophane package to be played with. Barbie doll. Barbarella.

Everyone wants to break the unbreakable girl inside of the human being. And drag tells us, that's not possible.

At the Back Door, everyone's favorite drag queen was Mahogany, a beauty with glittering legs that hadn't been seen anywhere since Annie Mae Bullock. She performed Beyoncé renditions, turning pirouettes, doing a full split. "End of Time," not even a popular track from Bey's 4 album, but I dream of how the queen resurrected it.

My favorite performer was a silent girl so mysterious no one had ever seen her out of her costume. She just appeared, in a black low-back Oscar de la Renta.

"I wonder," I muttered to a friend, "I wonder who her mother is." But what I meant was "Who is her daddy?" It was a notorious secret that many of the boys who were girls, and the boys who were beautiful, were funded by much older academics. I learned this the day I ran into a trans girl I'd see about town, an ebullient, brown-skinned Latina.

"Isn't it wonderful? My mister just bought this for me." I was surprised she stopped me; aside from the drag shows, we didn't know each other. It was an egg timer shaped like an egg. I didn't know how to be happy for her. But slowly, the stories of college tuitions covered and private jets started to make more sense to me. Trust fund fathers who lived on the periphery of the lake in the stoic wonder houses around the Brown County hills. They would lure them in first with small domestic tokens. They were rarely healthy lovers. One of the bartenders who ran the Back Door died that way. Olive. The cops team deemed it a suicide although he'd been known to drive to the woods and yell at the windows of a man he'd loved with his car parked in the mansion's roundabout. Maybe you can die of a broken heart. Maybe, but on with the show.

The Back Door was the brightly lit navel in Bloomington's underbelly, where street signs paid for by a sad Connecticut family asking, WHERE IS OUR GIRL?, slowly faded. There was one CCTV video of her crossing the street alone; the family refused to stop looking. When the parents and press finally got the police to dredge all the lakes to look for her skeleton, what they exhumed instead were eight heads—unidentified Asian men, their bodies never recovered. The records are public; the police never continued looking for them.

And the dance danced on. The cops knew that the Root

Cellar, the Back Door—and, by extension, Kirkwood Avenue and the bar Kilroy's—attracted all the young freshmen, the rooms packed with roofies. So much so that one summer the FBI distributed coasters that lit neon pink or green under ultraviolet, depending on the drugs, but what were the drugs I can't remember.

I can't remember. At some point, I was roofied too, at the Back Door. It was "an accident"; the lean grad school student I hung out with, who'd been lifting weights—my dance club partner for years—had written it off as an accident. All we remember is calling an Uber, too drunk to drive after just one cocktail. We woke up the next morning with sore legs; neither of us remembered how we drove home when we called each other the next morning. Through the forensics of the receipts we pooled together at Sunday brunch, we learned the car took us a block before we exited, fifteen minutes later. We had gotten into the car and headed back to the Back Door and ordered enough drinks to knock out a large barn animal.

On most nights, I stomped and tossed while a hot fat trans chick DJed. She wore neon and a Goth-style mullet. She always had a set that lined up the same hits. Charli XCX and Icona Pop. Whitney Houston, Madonna, Robyn. I'd stop to scream at the top of my lungs the lines that spoke the most to me, and stand in the middle of the dance floor imagining freedom. *I'm getting over you, I don't need anybody, I don't care,* I thought, was the blur from the sugar, and the drugs, and the blinding lights that made me a stronger person. We'd get lost in ourselves, then bump into each other and applaud each other's dance moves. There was always the ghost of some deep pain dancing alongside every one of us.

A friend of ours had been broken up with by his "daddy." He worked at the Kinsey Institute. I didn't know who Kinsey was. I'd just begun dancing with the idea that sexuality included a spectrum. He was hitting the dance floor hard. He wore earbuds and an iPod. I asked him to let me listen. He put the buds to my lobes; it was Mary J. Blige's "Not Gon' Cry." A slow one. He was tweaking, spanning circles with arms outstretched under the disco globe. I wondered which trust fund daddy did it.

I'd asked him once if it was the only Kinsey Institute in the world. He smiled and said, "Kinsey conducted all his research at IU Bloomington." I didn't know why he answered that way until I worked up the nerve to visit it. The archive room was tight and clean. Most of the things they stored you couldn't see without special permission. Figures. Fuck around and find out. He'd built a house for himself just off campus—brick by brick, the mortar oozing into the dining room. The elderly neighbors told cautionary tales about how Kinsey used to garden in a jockstrap. Up in the attic, he'd observe while his subjects, often students, engaged in all sorts of acts, sometimes with sheep. The neighbors claimed the place was haunted but I believe it was the whole damned town. Wretched, as a last-call bar, with the putrid scent of used young people. And the old men we never saw enter our dance floor, only the damage, their apparitions.

The dance dragged on. It grew blurred and unrelenting. Each time one more gilded flower seemed to lose the glow in their heart worth mentioning. Each time, the dance dredged up more gray. And on the night to end all nights, the mysterious girl in the platinum wig came in for a late-night drag show— her final performance.

Under a blue spotlight, she lip-synched like a revitalized Marilyn. The light danced around her sculptured face, in the prefecture of her bright red gloss. Her long slate gloves skimmed across her shoulders like architecture. How could anyone not love her, we all said, said of ourselves.

The rumor was she was headed to Los Angeles. That this was her last night in town before she was headed on tour or to do something big like the next *Drag Race*. Because what she was to us was an icon, we never knew her real name. Only a pseudonym. But as time dragged on we never heard from her again and we wondered, *Where did the unbreakable men leave her breakable body?*

PART III

I had a messy divorce. In this, I'm not alone, but divorce is such a lonely process. My wedding was a fairy tale. A long lace train, down under the Brooklyn Bridge, where my fiancé wore a suit he had custom-made to match what the Dutch prince wore at his royal wedding. On the day, he surprised me with a bouquet of flowers. I wasn't a froufrou girl at the time. I planned to walk down the outdoor aisle without them. But once, I'd randomly come across a picture in a magazine that looked like a meadow and a forest wrapped in old country twine and said, "Okay, this is a bouquet I could tolerate," and he remembered— that was seven months before we got engaged.

I was a Southern Christian girl. It was hard for my divorce not to feel like failure because, despite the fact I was nearly twenty-eight when I got married, my husband-to-be was my only—my wedding night, my first. So, when he admitted he'd been cheating on me throughout our courtship about a week into our marriage, I took the L and did my best to soldier on. I constructed it as my fault that I was in love and unhappy. And I assumed my husband loved me, and because he admitted to cheating, it must have meant that he had stopped. He hadn't. He didn't. Two years later, my sister found continued evidence of his infidelity in a Facebook post that popped up in the wee hours of the morning, something long since deleted by the time I woke up. She didn't tell me about it. She told him he had to. But the ultimatum didn't stick because he never did, I didn't know, and when my sister saw nothing changing in our relationship she started to resent me for being what she assumed was a delusional so-and-so.

My husband didn't confess to cheating again until he was actively pursuing a new woman, about six months later. We had this family rule where you could say anything and the other person wouldn't get mad if you said it in bed. The idea was, we'd stay in bed until we worked out the problem, because we wanted to always be friends. My parents hadn't been. So when I made that rule up I thought we'd use it to solve arguments about visiting my in-laws or leaving dirty socks on the carpet. I didn't expect my husband to stick his head under a blanket and squeak out some new betrayal like a naughty kid.

Naïve and trusting, I told him we needed to take this directly to the church. A Jehovah's Witness, I'd stayed chaste all those years because I thoroughly believed in the Scriptures, the sacrifices of Jesus, and the promise of a better earth. In fact, my husband and I were training to be missionaries, and planned to enter the service once I finished grad school. Surely, the elders in our congregation wouldn't want to see such a blight on cherished members of their flock. But institutions are institutions. I learned that the hard way. I knew the Bible backward and forward—honestly, back in the day I could have pimp-slapped you with a psalm—so I was shocked beyond mortality when the first spiritual heads we approached with my husband's problem told us this was "normal" for men sometimes and that I should just keep being a "good" little wife. *Pharisees*, I thought, remembering how Jesus knocked down the tables of the men collecting money at the door to his father's house. In this case, the price was my body, and I wouldn't accept it because it would mean to the blood of Christ the ultimate disrespect.

But I was poor and barely thirty. We had a condo and a car payment, but with me in grad school and both of us devoting full-time hours to our ministry, we were getting by on about $40,000 a year. Maybe an extra five grand in the years I won a few prizes for my poetry. And the rift my husband had intentionally caused between myself and my family was pretty irreparable. My divorce took time because I was nearly broke and alone.

I had two small indulgences at the time. The Nicki Minaj clothing line for Kmart, which could keep a girl in the Midwest looking pink and sexy for $17, and the random tchotchkes I'd snag from T.J. Maxx. One day, scouring the clearance aisles in a kind of blood-panic, I came across a Hula-Hoop. With an instructional DVD attached to it. *Why not?* I said to myself, although it's more likely I said *F——it*, since I'd been teaching myself to say one swear word a day—a task I practiced at home while washing dishes in the kitchen—my tiny rebellion against my former tribe. I purchased the hoop and took it home.

My new Hula-Hoop was soft and loud. It was as big as the dining table and covered in fuchsia neoprene. I'd been a clumsy kid, the kind who was teased because she could never keep the world in safe orbit around her body. I didn't expect to be good at this now, but that was precisely why it appealed to me. I was tired of how much goodness mattered in my pursuit of being a grown woman. In the midst of my divorce, the world owed me my lost girlhood. I took the cellophane off the DVD and balked at some white woman talking about "unlocking the goddess in you" while hooping beside a mountain in the intro credits. But, by the end of the first lesson, which was just passing the hoop from one hand to the other, I was hooked.

It felt good. I felt good. I had no other lover; I hadn't been able to pinpoint how much the infidelity had divorced me from my body. Whenever the blues started to creep over me, I would push some of the furniture out the way in our living room and lose myself in a wave of my own rhythm. In those few seconds I kept the hoop up, I felt beautiful. No competition. I felt flawless and earthy and privately mine.

My husband and I separated. When my mother and sister came to inspect the house, expecting it—and me—to be a wreck in the aftermath, they found the house clean, happy, a bouquet of flowers on the table, and the woman who never liked to be too girly girlishly excited to show off a new trick.

"Whoa ho ho!" my mom said. The ultimate compliment.

"Girl, it looks like you could be ironing laundry and cookin'

on the stove!" my sister joked. We all laughed as they continued to imagine scenarios in which I worked and werked a
hoop in motion—the balance of a Black woman's life. They
were proud of me. Although the conversations that would
come later about my impending divorce and decision to leave
behind our family religion would not be mild ones, my Hula-
Hoop tempered them with a sort of grace.

As evidence of the blessings of God, as I divorced my husband my life became rich and his a chaotic mess. He begged
to move back into the house during a winter when I'd be at an
Italian writing residency because he'd run out of friends'
couches on which to crash. In mercy, I said yes and packed my
hoops in my suitcase. By this time, I had allowed myself a collection of four, two of which could fold in ways that made
them portable for travel. It had been maybe four months since
I'd started hooping, but I'd become quite good. I'd advanced
to watching tutorials for tricks on YouTube, and treated myself to a slim gold speed hoop I had custom-made on Etsy; it
broke down into four pieces compact enough to fit in a carry-on
suitcase.

In Venice, I'd take my hoop out late at night and dance by
the canal's edge, its glimmer and wave synchronous with water. I ran through the city with the hoop across my shoulder
like a circus performer. Occasionally unleashing it to twirl or
lasso around my body in the empty streets when no one was
looking. Before my Hula-Hoop, I had never associated my

purpose with pleasure. With my own delight. If you knew me back then—I didn't even have the guts to say I made the cut in my top-ten list of favorite people. But in the months that followed returning home from hooping in Venice, I would lose the companionship of all of them: my mother, my father, my sister, my best friend—my husband. And staying inside the groove, staying inside the swirl of my own rhythm, kept me safe.

Around January 2—the anniversary of our engagement—my husband and I took a trip to Jamaica in an attempt to reconcile. Before we left, my mom and second church mom held an intervention trying to convince me not to go. They did not want me to divorce the man. But they were literally scared that if I went alone out of the country with him he might kill me. I couldn't understand the rationale. But it was a lack of balance I was accustomed to in the world outside of hoop life. By this point, I had graduated to spinning multiple hoops on my body at one time. I stayed in the flow. I trusted my gut. I stood up to my mother. She took a long time to forgive me. But I was a married woman who needed to see if there was anything redeemable in her Christian courtship. I owed this to the girl in me who had spent all those years doing her best to keep me safe.

The trip was disastrous. Naïve and trusting, I assumed we would use the time to align our values and recommit ourselves to the task of my husband's fidelity. He believed it was going to be a smoke-and-mirrors game. A romantic getaway where we went back to being the adventurous, carefree version of us other people envied. I wasn't having it. Pretension wasn't my kind of life. Lying on the beach next to him, trying to forget about him, I watched an old man pass by with gray dreadlocks and a handsome beard. A coastal activity coordinator.

"Miss, we're about to start a hula contest over there," he said, offering me a light blue hoop wrapped in a ribbon of turquoise cellophane. Having packed none of mine, I snatched the hoop out his hands. We contestants gathered: a scattering of kids, me, and a Jamaican sex worker (identifiable by the particular tattoo that adorned her thighs)—a woman who could actually dutty wine. The music started, and we all wiggled our hips.

After a few false starts, I tested the hoop's weight and width with my hands. It was a child's hoop, not built for a full-grown body, so I compensated in the spin by pouching my tummy out a bit, like a little kid. The move wasn't cute, but it was effective. The song reached its end and the kids had abandoned the competition in favor of using the hoops to beat each other over the top of the head. It was down to me and the sex worker, whose gorgeous hip-to-waist ratio made her a shoo-in to win. But what I had in my heart was the rhythm of life. I summoned it and went into my happy place, where nothing could hold me back and nothing but love surrounded me. While my competition tried to keep the beat of the music, I kept the speed of the space handed to me, the hoop, a whole entire life lesson. I kept hooping long after the music stopped. I didn't even notice the competition had ended. My worthy opponent came over and gave me the biggest hug.

"How'd you learn to move like that, girl?" she said, holding her weave back with both hands—the ultimate gesture of Black girl appreciation. I laughed.

"Girl, I am going through a terrible divorce!" We were still cackling when my husband walked up, shriveled and surly.

"Wow! You must be some type of gymnast or something," the bearded man said, shaking my hand as my husband approached.

My husband tried to say something—"Yeah, my w—"— but no one was listening. And from that day on, I danced for myself.

Online

Three days into the anniversary celebration for my dear friend Dorothée and my brain is short-circuiting. "Gratitude— Nueva Libertad" read the subject line to the email that had brought me here, folded my heart into a rush of golden violin strings. I couldn't understand a word of the email but the spaces that surrounded its exclamation points let me know it was typed fast, excitedly, floridly, as if worlds were going to converge, so I répondez si'l vous plaît'd and, right as spring ended, I was there. It was 2018, and my first solo trip abroad since divorcing was a French decade-anniversary party. How ironic.

My French isn't abysmal, it's nonexistent. We were staying, about fifty of us, at a castle an hour north of Avignon, a pleasant commune in southeastern France, in walking distance of the river. The landscape was unabashedly beautiful.

Blossoms and ivy burst from every crevice of the castle like ornate bouquets, and the grounds were covered in soft tufts of short-bladed grass that the children loved to roll and wrestle in. Each meal was an elaborately French multicourse affair, and we visitors would volunteer services as contributions, whether it be setting tables or braising things. Each night I was utterly overcome by how delicious everything had been, and how well organized, when no one I saw looked overly taxed or exhausted. One of Dorothée and her husband's invited guests was a classical circus performer. A man in his seventies. One night he donned lipstick and a pair of red, T-strapped, heeled Mary Janes and walked a tightrope he tied between two olive trees on the castle grounds. He offered a turn to anyone who wanted one. There were trios of guitar players at sunset. Dorothée's daughter wrapped herself up tight in my wide gray skirt until we looked like two tangled twins wearing the same robe. I loved being there. But I was mute most of the time and the quietness inside was getting to me.

I don't mind being quiet. I've developed a certain mastery over being quiet in big spaces because of how often I haven't known the language and been inundated with sounds I don't recognize. *Nod and smile*, I'd made my motto for most of my time in both Italy and the Netherlands. It wasn't that I was entirely speechless. It was just that I felt so comfortable with the ways I could break and build English at will that being less than fluent felt like such a letdown for me in worlds where I didn't want to function on a lower level. I wanted to be interesting. I wanted to be thoughtful. I don't know how to do that with a limited vocabulary.

Dinners were served family style on tables made with long wooden planks balanced on wine barrels, and the benches were planks balanced on cinder blocks. The china and earthenware serving vessels made the nights elegant, with the steaming dishes passing between the guests in an organized network. The event was meant to be social, an opportunity for all the channels that loved, formed, and supported the couple separately to gather as one unified river. But I didn't speak the language. I did as best I could for the first few nights to be as engaged as I wanted to be in the conversations by trying to piece together sentences made from cognates and words I understood. But by the third night, I couldn't keep up the façade. I pulled out my smartphone.

I'd probably pulled out my smartphone more times than I would admit. I had just finished being drawn into a conversation, in English, with a Frenchman and his Brazilian wife, who had dated in English and were much more apt to help me out with the endless stream of conversation that otherwise meant little to me. I pulled out my phone, unconsciously, still looking for that delicious break from live-processing people's comments, from the need to immediately respond. The hard click of my nails on the glass screen and the gratifying ping of finding a place to go that was voyeuristic—noisy with thoughts and images—but ultimately quiet. I was never very good at posting online, but I hadn't realized, in my shy moments, how much I'd come to depend on the habit.

I wasn't always like that. I remember years back, in the days when I met Dorothée, I wasn't a cell phone person. I was recently divorced, I was living in Portland, and the only thing I wanted to do was connect with people in a real way. I spent copious amounts of time going out to professional meetups and dance parties trying to find my people. I was always horribly frustrated that most of the meetups had become Facebooking and tagging a few photos of the group together before each person returned to the world on their screen, or dancing holding your phone up high over your head so people could see you having a good time on Snapchat. "I am right here," I said to the world, but the internet had become too loud for any of us to hear each other.

It was one of the things I loved most about Dorothée. She listened. She listened to all of us. The first time I met her, I was conducting an interview for the Portland Institute for Contemporary Art for the debut of her three-person show *Unwanted*. Rwandan, Dorothée was twelve in 1994, when her family fled the country to escape genocide. For the play, she returned to her home country as an adult to collect the stories of the women who were raped during the conflict and the children they birthed who lacked a place in any culture as the country did its best to hurry on, repair, and forget. The first time I spoke to Dorothée, we sat side by side, in line, on a bench in a small row. It was awkward to lay my smartphone down between us to record the conversation but easier to smell the heat of her body rising toward the stage, to take in the cameo of her profile, her immense beauty, to remember her. It was an unusual script for an interview but the perfect opening salvo to something longer, a friendship. I love her dearly, which is what made her worth traveling around the world for.

There's an irony to how easy it is for me to write down something I'm much too shy to say to someone in person. But that's probably a big part of why I'm a writer, lurking in the corners of someone else's happily-ever-after, and not off somewhere madly in love. In my heart, I'm always looking for someone to travel around the world for. I think this makes me an uncomfortable friend. I show up. That's how you know I'm serious about you. It rarely shows in what I say. I'm no good at small talk. I'm not good at surface relationships, the simple sugar of showing up and sharing pleasantries with people in ways that are sweetly compact and memorable. I only understand the hard duties. Scaling the rock of a mountaintop as we hold each other back to battle the wind. Few people are ready for that in their first or second passes at a new friendship. But Dorothée always was. And it made me feel loved by her in a way I've felt embraced by few people in practice.

She would send me photographs of her whole family floating topless on the French Riviera during their vacations. She would write to me on the anniversary of the genocidal murder of every girl in her Rwandan middle school before she would find herself a solemn place to cry, the only survivor.

Once, while I was coming home from yoga, caught under the awning during a rainstorm in Brooklyn, Dorothée sent me the most gorgeous message about an erotic dream she had of me where my sex turned into a hibiscus, a flower fragrant and ripe throughout Rwanda. I stood under the small vinyl shelter of the bodega entrance and cried. Boo-hooed. Wondering why it seemed nearly impossible for people to see me regularly and still love me with the same immense intimacy. I craved it. I needed it. Years later, I would tattoo a hibiscus in bloom onto my inner right arm, but in the intensity and confusion of my feelings, I didn't speak to Dorothée for months.

"You're addicted," said the Frenchman. He'd given up on trying to penetrate the cone of silence I was cultivating online, a bubble of memes, tweets, and droll English, amid the backdrop of this beautiful castle. I could almost hear him throw his hands up. His Brazilian wife was sitting next to me and I grazed her shoulder, nearly knocking over her wineglass, as I stared at my screen typing god knows what, trying desperately to connect. I tried to collect myself and return to the conversation of real life that had been open and waiting for me but had since moved on.

Sometimes I get stuck on what being "social" is or even

means in the world we've built now. Staying up with the times, whether it's online or in line, involves finding the right wavelength. It's fascinating to me how within the internet we've constructed a hub where people who aren't always thriving in a physical community, or can't, buzz like a hive. The white noise of billions of introverted strangers finding their voice, making their way, building game-changing moments in the space of a smartphone. Which is to say, to the Frenchman, I could have been doing something really important. I wasn't. Or was I? Because I had moved from the internet and started to think about how I wanted to write this essay—right here— reflecting on what I needed to do to truly consider myself a social person, someone in line with the times.

I've always considered traveling, even when solitary, a social activity—a chance to expand beyond what I've believed myself to be and see some fragment of the world differently. I believe that what's "social" is the things that change me. But I get a weird feeling when I admit to myself that's exactly what's social to me about "social media," it's changed me, and into someone I don't particularly like. What I don't like about social media is the demand to be interesting in two places at once—online and in the present—when where I live is really someplace much smaller, mostly in my head. I think about colors. I think about books I've read. What I've dreamed—I don't know how to turn any of these things into tagged dinner posts or dinner conversation but I have become addicted to trying, addicted to getting in line and getting things right. I hope if I open the right part of my chest someone will love me, as Dorothée made me feel, full of patience and slow to cast judgment.

Among the guests at "Libertad," there were about a handful of us Black women—a half-dozen or so, all of us from across the diaspora but mostly Francophone. Back at the party, my tiny dialogue with the Frenchman caught the attention of Penda N'Zi, a funny and pretty incredible, French-Senegalese playwright. Seated at the far end of the table, she stuck out her tongue, and I winked back. I scooted down to her end of the bench as the dinner plates were cleared and people opted in or out of the apple tart served for dessert. We sat with our legs straddling the bench so we could face each other—like two girls getting ready to play a hand game. But we traded stories instead of beats and rhymes.

We settled into a recollection of what introverted people did at parties before social media. She made me feel better. I hadn't thought that maybe the conflict with Libertad was me speaking in a different language and not speaking a different language.

"Smoked," said Penda. "Carried around big black cameras and took pictures of all the guests."

"I once went to a party in college where a friend pulled out an entire novel," I remembered. "I always carried a book."

"Or a journal," said Penda.

"It's what made me a writer. It was okay for me to pull out a journal and start writing at a party, like I was folding everyone there into history. Because I was there and I was recording, everyone was a part of it. People saw me as an artist, and so I felt like one."

I wonder what it takes now to become one. Even though online is where we're supposed to be, there seems to be a penalty in choosing the wrong time to document. I mean, who doesn't find influencers and wannabes pretentious? I do. The thing I don't like, even in myself, is the artifice that comes with setting up a scene.

On a nature walk the next day with a few of the diasporic women, we pass the most luscious field of poppies on the edge of the alps. I'm wearing one of my favorite outfits. Something I've had for years but now that I've filled out about thirty pounds fits differently and it pleases me. I think about a photograph I have wearing the same combo snapped naturally by an introvert with a large black camera on a Bloomington, Indiana, rooftop. I try to figure out how to ask one of the women I just met to snap a picture of me in a way that doesn't sound artificial. I'm tempted to overexplain. It seems too vain to just want a picture of myself surrounded in beauty, no matter the circumstance. But I'm thinking about how I could combine both photographs in a swipe-through post on Instagram and it feels incessantly stupid that this is what I do on my vacations. What did the man say? "You're addicted." I don't think it's addiction. I think it's anxiety. I'm afraid this is the only place I'll truly be seen, read. I'm so used to being unseen by the world—by majority culture—that now, given the chance to resolve that in a new world, on a new platform, I am overdoing it. I don't need to be online all the time. I just want to make sure someone notices me, closely, differently. Why am I looking for love online? Why do I think this is what love means?

I come from the America Online generation. MySpace. BlackPlanet. All these crispy little edges of the blogosphere. I have friends who still have friends they've chatted with for twenty years and never met in person. It's hard to say now that there's a higher value in all relationships that involve physical interaction, but I still feel the pressure to believe it, protect it. Although I love the veil that's lifted when we sit closer to each other on the internet than we do anywhere else. I like to believe it's not the posts we're addicted to, it's the conversation in the comments section, the possibility of DMs. The fact that we can live and thrive not just in the activities we share in our skins, but in the data that collects around the activities we share about our lives. The way we hone and harvest those events into hashtags to bring more of a like-minded flock into the fold. It reminds me of how seamlessly I've managed to communicate with Black people wordlessly while traveling. The nuances in our movements and glances forming a metadata we don't need to speak.

In my most romantic moments contemplating the internet,

I'm in love with the organism that surrounds the organism of our bodies. The multicellular collection of microcosmic breadcrumbs we leave behind, that organize like mycelium to tell the stories of who we are more intricately than we could ever describe ourselves. When I stop thinking about the data collected of our life online as an invasion of our privacy, I think about it as a multifaceted, categorical collection of everything we've been, everything we've done, everything we've asked to become. Not just in the collection of what we share, but also in the recognition of what we respond to and who calls out to us. I, like most of us, have only the most basic relationship to its inner workings, but there's something that I see of our life online when, in the real world, people congregate to make the interstitial happen. A snapshot, some hashtags, a geotag. The archetypes we inhabit now and keep building beyond imagination. I wonder what the difference is between being addicted to being online and being obsessed.

As far as the staged photograph, where I look like a curvy Black Heidi in a long floral skirt and graphic bra top, it didn't matter what the story was I wanted to communicate or its intended audience. It never does. What mattered, what I remember, was the women who surrounded me in the moment could understand me—their English no more certain than the Frenchman's. Before I could jump into my apology for my attention-seeking—why I would want a picture of me in this beautiful scenery, knowing I would post it—they were setting up the perfect angle and trying to decide if I'd look best with the blossoms alighting everywhere in my hair. Their French clicked above me like a network of code constructed to build a snapshot, not unlike the web that repositioned Dorothée's romp on the French Riviera into the "Received" folder of my Gmail. Physical or digital. The vectors that bring us together like lines guiding travel on a map.

On nuance: there is a way Black people speak to each other that always reminds me of the internet. It's like we open up within each other a search engine of possibility. Aside from the fact that our cultures are such hubs of culture (music, food, idiom, dance), what we're expected to know of everyone else's culture in life in the wider world is like this Google search that keeps refining itself beyond language.

"Well what about . . . ?"

"And if we . . . ?"

"Wouldn't that remind you of . . . ?"

"Yes, in '96 or 2016?"

"God, yes. The best album?"

I'm making this up. I know so little French, but as the women compose a dialogue around how to snap the picture I've asked for, I sense my algorithmic search come into focus. Soon the words that are absent in dialogue become more powerful than the words I can't translate. I learn so much about us in those moments. Who loves stand-up comedy. Whose vintage Instagram shop sells gorgeous rattan handbags. Who's a dyed-in-the-wool, die-hard hip-hop fan. It isn't the stuff that is explicit that comes out in what we don't say. What comes out is the framework of who we are. To me, the structure upon which our life online hinges: what we listen for; what we're looking for.

We snapped the photo. It only took minutes, the walk back to the castle much longer, but I can't help but indulge in the meta-dialogue. It delights me, the play between being online and in line, which will inevitably make much of the future. I think we're afraid of an end to reality as we know it, of having the virtual consume us, but in my least cynical moments I wonder how we will adapt to the ability to be known in wider angles, especially for those who are currently marginalized due to physical, social, or other circumstances, especially people of color.

Sometime after lunch, a group of French Libertad attendees asked us to come with them to the river and we said, "Oui." It was a beautiful romp, all honeyed and golden. Ten of us running through the satisfyingly dry crack of brush to the babbling lip of the river. A hive mind. At its edge, we found a set of rocks and awkwardly sunbathed, rolling up sleeves, pant legs, or skirt sheaths to get in a little extra sun. At least the Black girls did. The French kids were already tearing off their clothes, plunging into the muddy sludge of the bank and coating their skins with it—a primeval self-care routine that baffled me. They were surprised we didn't take our clothes off.

Taunted us, even. In English, as if I weren't the only one for whom French was a foreign language, pedantically reassuring us that it would be "okay" if we branched out.

"You're _____."

When I think about search engine optimization, I often think about the snap judgments white people make, no matter the country, without reading the context. People who feel like all culture is their own (and not a multiplicity of data culled and harvested into categories, and subcategories . . .) draw the dumbest conclusions.

"Don't be scared!" a Frenchwoman cried out to us from the bank, likely commenting on our modesty, her neck and belly covered in river clay that cracked and peeled in the sun like a scorched earth.

"You don't know what you're missing!" a man cried out. Yes, we did. Each of our brains running through a catalog of search engine results for "the history of exoticized naked Black bodies" and "shallow-water parasites." The risk and the spectacle. At this point, we've already cataloged all of these struggles online. On TikTok, Facebook, Twitter, and Instagram. We've explained what we are actually missing—a place where our bodies can exist, without judgment, without fear. What we are "missing" is freedom. We know that. But why we're still missing it after we've provided ample instruction into what we need, across all forms of media, still baffles me. It struck me most in the presence of Dorothée's friends because her work, as an activist and playwright, is dedicated to telling those stories about us—the survivor stories of victims of genocide, the collective voice diversely black and culturally Black women and nonbinary people are forging across the world. In this moment, when I was being asked to disrobe in front of strangers, I had to ask myself: *Have any of these people ever seen Dorothée's work?* Not because I was looking to them for some sort of "wokeness," but because it didn't seem to occur to them that the work she made rendered her part of a group. A class of international, intellectual, artistic leaders who were as Black as Dorothée was. We all used media to disrobe, as much as we could, for Eurocentric audiences. So it wasn't going to be our practice to do so on holiday, for a group of French people who thought they needed to lead us toward the promised land of progressiveness.

See, they read us wrong. They summed up all they knew about Black identities and assumed our choices came down to some moral code—the modesty of our Muslim and Christian upbringings, our immigrant and outsider statuses. But that wasn't it. I recognized—thinking about all the nude saunas I'd visited in the Netherlands, the only Black person in hundreds, and about the topless pictures Dorothée sent me of her family's sailing trips around the Riviera—each of us might have made different decisions to get naked individually than what we were called upon to make as a group. The group's purpose was to protect the free choice of even the least of us—on "our side" or "theirs"—to create a counter-resistance for those who might not feel entitled to speak up. It's the way we are networked.

In my travels, I've noticed that white locals like to assume the reserve they notice in the people they consider the cultural fringe comes from an inferiority of experience. That, somehow, in our avoiding the spaces in which they feel most affirmed, we're denying ourselves the opportunity to feel we're a part of something. In reality, what they've missed is that many of us have moved on from feeling we need to be a part of the dominant conversation. That we have comfortably carved out our own. So comfortably, in fact, that our connection goes beyond shared age, language, socioeconomic background, or ability. This was the passport "whiteness" was meant to offer to all people of less melanated skin. A stamp of security. The stamp of the majority. But it hasn't proved the case when it comes to whiteness and traveling.

If I arrived at "Nueva Libertad" as a white American who didn't speak French, the French would have made no efforts to include me in their ranks because of our shared "whiteness." I would have had one choice: acclimate or have a miserable time. Whereas, the quiet beauty of black travel is that, throughout the globe, black speaks to each other through what we've shared on social platforms. We've inadvertently built communities on common wavelengths, bonds that are stronger than geography or language. This is the kind of shared community "white" people assumed they were creating for themselves when they left behind their rich cultural ethnicities for social power. But because the power of "whiteness" is based on exclusion (who I think you aren't) and not inclusion (all the things I believe you can be, and will be, and have to teach me), it's not real solidarity. It doesn't travel well.

The closest parallel I can come to about what it's like to be in sync with the African diaspora while traveling abroad is the feeling many marginalized people today find being online. But for Black people, that feeling of being seen and being heard can exist for us in a world beyond the screens—probably more for us than anyone. If you understand blackness, you can travel anywhere in the world and be safe, make friends, and find enlightenment. Who you are can be all you need, because we are a network of resources linked together in ways that the dominant culture ignores. If I am addicted to anything, it's this: searching for a world I can be in the flow with IRL, inasmuch as I was with the group of artists and liberators I gravitated to at Nueva Libertad at crucial moments. Saying our "skin color" united us is reductive. None of us were the same shade of brown or came from the same ethnic background. But what we shared among each other was decades of YouTube music videos and Google searches of key terms, of finding answers to questions of who we are leading us to the same online materials. Media moguls like to make us believe that living is decided by who subscribes to the dominant culture, but we make all the content. The dominant culture tries to convince us we are "missing out," but when we opt out of their social platforms, they are the ones who have nothing to say. The world online has dramatically upgraded the power of marginalized people in the real world. But the people who've always been comfortable going outside don't want you to know this, because they don't want to interrogate the quality of their own experiences. For so long, those people who've been able to go outside and get naked with no fear have held those rights above the rest of us as a right to the whole world. Not anymore. When my new friends and I said "no thanks" to their freedom, we forced them to open their own search engines and ask, "Why not?" I saw their faces, buffering . . .

Much of the crew who covered themselves with mud that day did end up sick with a parasite. From this, I learned one thing: belief that there is something freeing in being a part of the status quo is a dangerous idea. At best, it's stagnant. At worst, it could cost you your very life. Because the world isn't just organized by those at the top anymore. Because of the internet, we are all always simultaneously invisible and being surveilled. This is a simple fact that those of us on the outskirts can never ignore and those who felt safety in their power-majority status have had to rethink since the pandemic. That nakedness that felt private, primal, and privileged to our French friends no longer belongs to any of us, in any context. We are always "online." We are always one photo away from being exposed, or one geotag from being found. There is very little distance between the life we live online and the life we live outside it. We are all "addicted." The question is, will that make us more aware—for the better—of how our online communication affects our very real lives? That, in the presence of a "social" media, where we show up and how we show up is always political? (Use your nakedness wisely.)

In understanding what it means to have a "social media," a network of mass communication forged through membership in lots of individual societies and not just one, integrative thinkers are more prepared for the broader world. Because of our circumstances, there are more integrated minds today than ever before. More and more people who are "missing out" by the system's standards are finding ways to restore their power by organizing through online channels. There is power in the people who show up in the comments and not the pictures. In the people who are the "virus" that makes viral content. In the Twitter hashtags, the Reddit threads, and the heavily annotated notes on Genius. There is something to getting addicted to the conversational styles of the future. There is something to how being online liberates the ways we understand each other for how strange, and specific, and peculiar we are. Of course, that's not always the case. But I wonder what would have been different about the things our French friends felt we were missing had they been privy to our dialogue just a few hours earlier. Seeing how connected we were through the knowledge we shared, and how it broadened the data we had to query from when making decisions.

In this world, I wonder what it's like to only be responsible for knowing one set of facts. To never have to question whether the choice you make, based on how you feel, is the right one. Does that life feel as unfree as it reads? There is a lack of wisdom, a lack of basic machine learning, in this reliance on the unbroken dominance of the majority that will make "the majority" extinct. French or otherwise. It's inevitable. If not from covering themselves in parasitic clay found on the edge of still riverbanks, then from missing the opportunity to learn more from those they categorize as outliers.

When we get past the privacy issues, what's beautiful about our inter-networking in the internet is that we all exist as a network of decisions. I love to visualize it as the singularity of our physical bodies surrounded by all the choices we make, online and off, that build us into archetypes. There is no majority in this world. Only the mycelium of the people we desire to be, and hope to be, and want to appear to be, mixed in with the architecture of who we are. Which, in my mind, at this point, can be deduced into two things—the questions we ask and what we search for. Relegating any algorithm to a single interval, one unquestioned idea, will kill it eventually.

We need the conversation beyond majority belief for an idea to survive online. We need interrogation in this world, not just assumption.

The trek back to the castle from the river was long, dirty, and tiring. But, after dinner that evening, we danced. Our universal coded language. The songs were DJed, a few people accompanying with drums, and Dorothée at the center of all the dark-skinned women she'd congregated waving like a flag of justice. We worked our bodies around the hub of her, the zeitgeist, without a care for how we showed up in the world at that moment. We were the world wide web, our origins from different parts of the Continent and beyond, spawning out, our movement infectious. I turned around and danced in a tiny triangle with the Brazilian woman and her French husband, humming like lightning bugs under the buzz of the string lights that kept the castle lit as a city all night.

On Them

I'm standing outside on tiptoe trying to find clear reception in a New England valley. Dorothée has called me from France. She's seen something on my social that she wants to discuss: the fact that I've changed my pronouns.

"Tell me all about it," she says, and I feel butterflies, like I'm opening, like a new book. I tell her about all the places I've traveled. All the places I've been to—not on a map but in my mind. The truth is I've been puzzling through how to define my identity for a very long time. Asking myself, at such an advanced age, is it even a question, really, and does using a pronoun define you? I look at my reflection on the phone. I've always been distinctly feminine. But, since the time I had my first boyfriend at nineteen, I've been puzzling over what to call my body. We were a unique pair. A Catholic school boy of

Eastern Kentucky stock growing out his regulation crew cut into a look regularly sported by a stigmata Jesus, me with dark skin and the curly hair I would eventually trim down to a faux-hawk. We were playing with gender back then and we didn't even know it. Or of course we did. It makes a lot of sense to me that my first love was also the first person to introduce me to trans culture. *Hedwig and the Angry Inch.* Not a perfect rendition, but the first time I watched the bildungsroman on-screen I teared up seeing my truth and realizing, I have been comfortable being a girl but not a woman.

There's a certain neutrality in childhood, an ambivalence to the future, a carelessness about the proper alignment of sex organs. So for the longest time, while I was young, it made the most sense to me to imagine my gender as a rock star—David Bowie, Grace Jones—someone alien, androgynous, and more concerned with space than location. But here was the boy, the first person I loved, and the romance seemed to define my certainty that I was growing into a woman.

But at the same time, I hated being sexualized in that way. My body felt more like a bird than a lotus, wings on both front and back from which I wanted to either shield my eyes or float away. My curves were setting in. The low-waisted jeans I wore that were in fashion beveled angles at my hips and formed a sharp, shadowy V where my pelvis protruded. The combination confused me. I was skinny, but I didn't expect my lower sex to start bulging into a mound someone would notice. I was a virgin. I didn't have a clear vision of how my body should be building itself. Our Southern Christian upbringing kept him and me glued together until we could sort what to do with one another. Our faithfulness gave me time to blame chastity for my lack of intercourse, and ignore that I was benignly frightened of the lower half of my body.

In divinely profound ways, we connected. We did art projects, collages—cutting and pasting—kissed each other topless. When he fell in love with a film, he'd play it for me on the big projector screen of an abandoned classroom. *Hedwig* took us both back to our childhoods. And finally, someone else whose gender was rock star let me fall in love with me too. It was not only that Hedwig's story was trans and nonbinary, it was that it recognized the complexity of one's gender within gnosis, a Greek word meaning "knowledge." It wasn't just gender I felt conflicted by, but the knowledge of it. I had to conceal my contradictions; I felt sexier in a pair of X-large Spider-Man Underoos than anything else. I felt perverse, as if I was trying to reclaim my childhood, as if I hadn't finished because I was still trying to grow into something else.

I had not finished growing up. I watched Hedwig sing "The Origin of Love." I cried. I saw, in its retelling of mythology, what the gods had done to me, split my perfectly round wholeness into parts. "Children of the moon," Hedwig called us—

those who were part son and part daughter. The pretext of the narrative was that, on earth, we're here looking for our other halves. How we search for that love in another person, only to realize that the search itself has made us whole. Hedwig falls in love; she takes down the rock star she builds into her avatar, Tommy Gnosis, to become both of them. "To know that you're whole."

I say to Dorothée, "them" for me was a spiritual journey. The closer I got to being comfortable with my earthly form, the more I understood its multiplicity. Its merger of the Divine Masculine and Sacred Feminine—or vice versa, it doesn't really matter which. The longer I live, the more I see the reality that we are wider than language, and in pursuit of that vastness, some of us struggle to find connection. This wasn't a conversation I expected to be having with myself at forty. I thought I'd left self-discovery behind in my college years, but I grew up in a time and place where the search for who I was ended with watching *Hedwig* and a lot of *E! True Hollywood Story* television documentaries on hermaphrodites. I was twenty-one when, after a couple of readings through the novel *Middlesex*, I became brave enough to ask my mother whether or not my sex had been altered at birth. She said, "No!" with surprise, assuring me, "You are all woman." I think she assumed I felt bad about my body, because I was small and didn't look as womanly as I might have desired. But I was looking for the reason why I felt liminal—not because I was unhappy with my body, because I was happy with the ambiguity. I didn't want to leave that ambiguity behind.

I'd been menstruating since I was a preteen. I understood cognitively I had to be female, but it's important to see that gnosis is the noun "knowledge" and not itself knowledge. I did not "know" myself because I could not see myself in a woman's form, someone defined by a particular femininity. But I didn't know it was normal to feel that, to question what so many people seem to know with such certainty. As time went on, it became easier to be a woman. The language was simple; I picked up a performance of gender and eased my way into it. I played around a lot with the affect of a pinup girl. To think of this as discovery, play, to give it kinship with the dress-up of childhood, made it easier to be ultrafeminine, because it was like drag—make believe, fantasy, a footnote. A commentary on the society that dictated that I was a Southern woman.

By the time I became a housewife, the performance was rote; being a woman didn't feel real, so I stopped thinking about what wasn't real. And for a while, I just lived without that sense of reality. But as time went on I realized finding my other half, my origin point, grew increasingly difficult because I couldn't figure out where I felt whole. I stopped worrying about it until I went back to college.

To teach this time. To be taught—teaching in America today is an education in pronouns. Pronouns have become part and parcel of youth and, in some ways, outpaced the correct pronunciation of "ethnic" first and last names. That's why it was difficult for me to understand the movement in the beginning. The multiplicity of gender constructions, at the outset, looked to me like something rich white New England college kids had invented to make themselves more marginalized than poor kids, and Brown kids, and the myriad other underrepresented kids. That frustration was commonplace in my early undergraduate teaching days and manifested in conversations like this one.

During my first year teaching, a student listed as "Thomas" on the student roll sheet asks me to use the name Rachel. "My pronouns are 'she/her' or 'they,'" Rachel tells the class. Rachel's countenance reminds me of Moby on the cover of his *Play* album, a work unabashed in its Black appropriation. It's hard for me to "see" Rachel in the way I want to, since her voice is her most dominant feature. In my class composed mostly of BIPOC Amherst College first-year students, Rachel is a senior from another campus. Her presence intimidates her peers as the oldest, whitest, and male-est voice in the class. One day in workshop, I slip and call her "them" instead of "she." She emails me claiming I misgendered her. But I didn't. I said "them" instead of "she" in recognition of the multiplicity, consciously. I've got a Southern lilt. I might have swallowed my consonants. "'Em" sounds a lot like "him" to someone used to defending a fixed position, to someone from

New England. Southern tongues are more mutable by definition (*You coming over the house with Joffrey 'n' 'em?* Not a New
England sentence.) I'm not upset at standing corrected. I was
frustrated by the ways she represented the dominant culture,
even in her concerns about bias. Even when I made an effort,
I was patronized and misread. I apologized, although in my
heart I felt adamant she had announced her openness to
"they" as a pronoun. "That's okay," she said, "I've done nothing but act and dress AMAB in class." I googled the abbrevia-
tion and smiled. "Assigned male at birth." *Thank you, Rachel,*
I said to myself with utmost sincerity. She educated me. *Trans
people do not owe you their gender performance. Nonbinary people don't owe you their androgyny.* I started to recite this to myself as a newly learned gospel. But this didn't stop me from
needing to blow off steam with a set of BIPOC UMass graduate students I'd befriended. I had met them at a poetry reading I'd done that summer in New York.

"Text us if you ever need to know where to get good ethnic
food," the biracial woman of the pair told me. Frustrated with
my class that day, I rang them up and we met at a local coffee
shop.

"She said I misgendered her, but I didn't. I wouldn't be of-
fended if I hadn't consciously tried to make sure I respected
her pronouns. And I did. But there isn't the space in this conversation for me to say that." The moment reminded me of

how I've been tempted to misgender people who have been racist to me to engender an honest dialogue—tempted to, but never have intentionally done. I know how hard the fight for visibility has been as someone Black and not-straight in the academy. But I didn't take kindly to my allyship being ignored, simply because they—as college students—assumed I'd react differently, especially when I was spending my free time with them instead of my colleagues.

It wasn't just my first year as a full-time college professor, it was also my first year living in New England. Despite being Black, I didn't read as "liberal" enough in Amherst. And I didn't want to. Because, particularly in the politics of New England colleges, radical and liberal are two very different agendas. Living in an often self-aggrandizing, predominantly white, neoliberal town, I was uncomfortable with how often the conversation of college-wide gender tolerance superseded all other cultural ones. My girl students were still being sexually threatened, my Black students were still being assaulted by the n-word, and my students who represented everything in between were offered even fewer resources for conflict resolution, as if nothing in the landscape had changed since the days Emily Dickinson walked the campus. I'd left corporate America to become a professor in hopes this would be a place I could develop real dialogue between myself and the next generation. But *"hope" is the thing with feathers*, the Amherst bard once mentioned, and I held that bird close to my chest. The assertiveness around using the correct pronouns felt like rainbow-washing on top of the abundant whitewashing that was already being done to a campus named after the man who gave smallpox blankets to Shawnee and Lenape citizens. The fact that Amherst, named for one of America's earliest bioterrorists, wanted to get fussy about grammar when most of its students couldn't name the Indigenous tribes whose land they sat on was absolute absurdity to me. But I didn't want confirmation of my opinions, I wanted a conversation.

I wanted a place where I could establish a dialogue beyond the muddy grayness of this new language territory. I wanted real college bipartisan dialogue. But the student I attempted to start that with tried to start a rumor that I was transphobic. It didn't stick, there was no logic for it to adhere to.

I won't lie, this made me angry. I was an outsider marginalized in my own right, but there was a liberal New England tendency for the privileged to act more injured than another more vulnerable party. The calluses came off my own injured ego when I watched another student, Black, assigned male at birth, my graduate apprentice, approach intrepid conversations about gender while in the process of transitioning. He was my TA. I was growing increasingly annoyed that at the beginning of each session he would interrupt by jumping into the lesson in order to call roll and ask that each student repeat their pronouns. I assumed he was being overly cautious. That caution sometimes felt like bullying. Aside from the prejudices I was facing as a new professor of color, I grew up with educators who barely got my first name right—and my name is Irish. But I was also grappling with my own truth. *What are my pronouns? What* are *they?*

Each week, my TA would begin class by stating his name and offering up his pronouns as "he/him," instructing the class to follow his model. And I would say the same thing every class period: "Hello, my name is Shayla and you can call me Professor Lawson." I refused to offer up a pronoun option. My TA's insistence upon asking felt like an indictment because, truthfully, referring to myself as "she" in front of a group felt completely wrong.

"You know we don't have to do this," I said to him one day after class. I'd come to know him better by then, as someone wonderfully astute and soft-tempered. I assumed I was opening up a conversation freeing him from the burdens of being politically correct for liberal white academia. He knew what I meant. We didn't have to cater to whiteness. *We* didn't have to do this for *them.* He thanked me politely. The following week, he attended class in a dress.

"My pronouns are 'they/them,'" "he" said to the class for the first time, after months of leading roll call. And now I understood what they'd been working up the courage to do all semester, introduce themself to us. The dress, an intentional part of the introduction, looked unwieldy on their body. I was tempted to say, once more, "You don't have to do this"— referencing their demonstrative change in dress, not their shift in pronouns. But I saw something in their eyes. That they were on a new journey, something intrepid. That identifying as nonbinary, in a Black "male" body, as an authority figure, was an essential part of their activism. A way of announcing the balance they now sought in their personhood. A chance to reclaim the inherent femininity they so desired to be at the forefront of who they were as a person. A duality that would always be lost to them as long as my classroom—the world— only saw them as a "Black man," one rigid, homophobic, hyper-masculine stereotype. How incredibly difficult to be a leader while in the process of your own discovery. How brave to al-low yourself to be.

When we don't ask people's pronouns, we risk a lot more than misgendering them. We miss the opportunity to correct any misconceptions we may have about how people see them-selves in the changing world, as they continue to educate themselves and realign their values. We miss the chance to rectify a dying system that dictates "men" one way and "women" the other, asking us to utterly deny how far we've come from those antiquated notions when we look at what people are actually doing in the twenty-first century, how we are actually living. Our world has grown diverse and broad. Redefining boundaries is what's become interesting to us.

Not reinstating traditions that didn't have our best interests in mind to begin with. I know what that's like, just from trying to be a "woman" as a Black person. In the simplest of terms, one of the things that's supposed to define my "womanhood" is being frail, or "soft." But I'm a Black woman. "Strong" is the only word that's put in front of my "womanhood" with any proudness or regularity, a word completely counter to what "womanhood" is. A modifier that excluded black women full citizenship in womanhood for centuries, our bodies and personalities often described by how "unfeminine" we are. I didn't choose to be a "she." And in American culture, I've never had the chance to be one. And that's just one small part of my own personal journey that "she" doesn't cover. As conversationally simple as our world looked before preferred pronouns, it was denying more people agency than we ever thought about.

I see the acceptance of pronoun usage as similar to how we've accepted stars. They fire billions of light-years ahead of us in a shape we cannot ascertain, and yet we've come to learn they are more than just those specks of light we see in the dark. We do not have to be in the dark. In time, we will no longer let our eyes be the limit of how we perceive people. I know we can learn this because we are getting there with nationality. We've gotten pretty good about calling out classless people who still ask a stranger, "What country are you from?," immediately rendering them as different. The broadening of gender identity is asking us not to make the same mistake of familiarity we used to make with foreignness. He, she, they, or otherwise, it is asking us all to become more knowledgeable about ourselves.

I didn't expect teaching to open up old wounds, old songs, reminding me of where I had been cut apart and unstitched by planetary fissures. As I opened myself up to more curiosity about myself, I watched the queer community of the valley and grew inspired. There were novelists, poets, and professors throughout the five-college boroughs who had wrestled with gender, struggled with gender, and found humility in the constant rediscovery of oneself instead of narcissism—something other than a need to be more than what God allotted. But, like the Bible says, "male and female He created *them*." I think about the messengers—the angels—who were never binary in structure; a messenger is what I've become. I don't mind the ways I will always look two-dimensional to certain people. I will always be a Black woman; black people have always existed outside the binary since its inception. The gender boundaries of a patriarchal, capitalist, colonial system have always denied us our full personhood. Black women are chastised for their power because it's "unladylike." Black men are thrust into tropes of hypermasculinity and punished for showing any softness. Aside from troubling the waters of Christian creation myths, our adoption of "they" reclaims the agency we need as inherently nonbinary beings caught in a spiritually corrupt system. They reclaims our divinity. They acknowledges the ways black people have been denied completeness in a corrupt framework. They gives the choice of who we are back to us. I'm a Black woman and a black woman. I'm not striving to be a "woman"—someone whose gender adheres to a racist white cultural construct. I refuse that which doesn't suit me, understanding myself wholly perfect in design, believing instead in the freedom for all people to be comfortable in their skins. Free spirits are never binary. Identifying myself as outside the system that has marked us is not a division of my spirit but a realigning of it.

Contemporary culture didn't make me a nonbinary person. I inherited it by learning more about where my ancestors came from. "Them" isn't a new phenomenon. Much of non-Western culture has always had a place for gender beyond biological sex, with names for people whose gender expression did not conform to sex, people whose sex belonged to no specific gender, and Two-Spirit people, whose journeys on earth reflected a biological and metaphysical balance. In light of *our* many forms, there are many languages that developed without the use of gendered pronouns altogether. There are whole histories on earth separating gender from sex, leaving gender a question of semantics—not nature.

"Yes," Dorothée said during our call, "that's how it was for us at home in Rwanda. 'He,' 'she,' those were for me more of a French convention. No wonder so many artists, Black women in particular, are rethinking how we refer to ourselves."

If we think of the meanings within "them," the meanings compose the circle of love's origins finding completeness. Not in other people but in ourselves. Like Hedwig's rock ballad "The Origin of Love," we're the children of the sun, Earth, and moon stitched back together, beyond our genitals. Comfortable in our bodies. Finding other places where their truths bear fruit. The transition to use new language is particular, easy to misunderstand or mock, but doesn't every new word taste funny until it doesn't? So many of the people I know are looking more deeply at who they are and what part language plays in that, people of all ages and genders. One of the most surprising experiences I've had in the process of changing my pronouns is hearing "Thank you" from a former student of mine, whom I love like family. Mika was trying to say as much to me when telling me the change felt "important." I got nervous, because I assumed what was meant was that the change was important to this era. I tried to backtrack until—

"To me," Mika said, "the change was important to me." It was important to them that I changed my pronouns, because for years, since their family had moved from the Philippines, they'd struggled with American womanhood. "I didn't feel like a person in English," they said. In Tagalog, the pronouns for "him" and "her" are the same, making personhood genderless. I am learning this is true for many languages, among them Chinese, Kinyarwanda, Estonian, Finnish. That the fixed notion of "he" and "she" I grew up with, speaking English as an American, is a myth. Much like me, there are people all over the world who have integrated themselves into western European language traditions, and have been forced to adopt a gender status in the process. Ascribing to themselves a binary that is foreign to them. Abandoning the clarity they found in one common pronoun for "a person." The modern question of pronoun usages is not just a conversation about self-actualization, it's a battle about who gets to define language. And, in our contemporary times, if English is meant to maintain its function as a "universal" language, it will have to adapt to function in the more equitable world we are building, not just the colonial one it forged.

I write because when language adapts we let the world in. But humanity can only grow if we're as fluid in flesh and blood as we are in ink. But first, there are the words, I am finding the words to get to the bottom of how I decolonize myself. And when the language fails my quest for freedom, I make it my choice to question it. I see the "they" in me as not unlike the X in Malcolm. Marking what we have discovered on the path toward the divine. I will never be mainstream, I will never fit the binary. I don't want to. I don't need to make my identity an audacious battle, it already has been. In "they," I am claiming that I will honor where being myself has gotten me and will not be enslaved by the models that force me to conform and obey, without question, again.

On the last night I lived in Amherst, I was so severely incapacitated by an injury I sustained on campus, I couldn't walk. I didn't know this was the precursor to years of heartache and hardship, of accepting disability as another way I'd have to interrogate the very fabric of being. I didn't know the questions about personhood I was beginning to ask would change my very life. But what I do know is, it was the people of the Pioneer Valley who opened my eyes and set the tone for my self-discovery; I'm grateful for that. Despite my best efforts to be "normal," I wasn't, and was running embarrassingly late to a dinner in Northampton—my body just couldn't get up to speed with where my mind was. I texted my dear friend Michael, a professor in the Russian Department, a profuse set of apologies.

"Don't worry. We have a lifetime together," he wrote back. Seeing those words from a friend when I was in the midst of a major life transition freed me. I felt unburdened of the prevailing cultural stigma that I be simple, easily categorized, manageable—no matter what the circumstance. I heard, in those words, the confirmation that the process of being known was meant to be a long one. Like learning. Like healing. A lifetime.

I still believe that the pursuit of knowledge is one of the

strengths of academia. But personal inquiry is happening in spaces beyond its cultivated walls. The interrogation of pronouns isn't just a liberal college agenda. It's evidence that our modern quest for equity has extended beyond the titles assigned to us at birth, and will continue to be examined by this next generation well past a few curious years surrounding their adolescence. "Them" is just the beginning. We have a lifetime to figure ourselves out. Even if you feel your gender is fixed, look again. Because, no matter what you've been told, the world's definition of gender has no fixed position. Depending on where you are, you too may be a very nonbinry entity, and that's all right. In traveling, most of my greatest awakenings have come through the struggle of reintroducing myself to who I thought I was. Hello: from the forty-something someone who identifies as rock star. Hello: to whoever you are to yourself.

On Femme

Cairo, Egypt

One of my wildest memories of traveling is my trip to Cairo. Cairo is a place I chose to go because two of my friends were visiting me during the spring break of my study abroad in Venice. And although they'd obviously come for the Italian experience, I couldn't see spending my free week somewhere where I couldn't have a broader one. So Egypt is what we booked: the library of Alexandria, a ride on camels through the pyramids, and a Hyatt right along the Nile River. In about a week, god bless.

I was still at that phase in my life where I felt like travel was really more an accumulation of what you did than who you spent your time with. Nowadays, the idea that two of my girl-friends would come all the way overseas to see me would be enough. But I was still engaging in guerrilla tourism—See everything! Do as much as possible!—as fast as I could. After a few days in Venice, where the girls bought beautiful boots, took afternoon pausa, and dined on pasta, we were boarding a flight to Cairo. We had no idea what to expect. Friends in our Bible study group had recently gone on the same itinerary— an Indian man and his blond Wisconsinite wife. We'd Skyped. They talked about how cool it was to walk around like celebrities in Khan el-Khalili market—people stopping to take their photographs and asking them to sign things in English script. I was skeptical of the couple's "celebrity" status in an international city, two Midwestern tourists in the Middle East, but I didn't write it off.

I reported this back to my girlfriends. They were fascinated. Ashiwa was a half African American, half Sudanese Louisville local. Dawn's family was mostly from outside of Boston, but were known around our hometown—Lexington, Kentucky— because they were a large family who all sported the same signature gap between their front teeth, a West African sign of beauty. Ashiwa and Dawn were both just shy of five and a half feet and curvy. Beautiful women, but not the kind who got attention in the towns we were from, with their debutante balls and horse culture.

It was a fate I knew well until my study abroad in Italy. I'd never considered myself attractive living in Kentucky. I was skinny, with big eyes, an Afro tuft of hair crowning my nape and ears. When I moved to bigger cities, I was mistaken for a model, but in Lexington, the question I got most often was "Why don't you go to the beauty parlor" or "the Clinique counter, like your sister?" My sister was such a feminine beauty that, by high school, on one trip to Atlanta, she'd been asked out by Drake—canvassing the food court of Lenox Square mall before his *Take Care* album—and stopped by a *Jet* photographer to see if she wanted to be "Beauty of the Month."

Black beauty is a different feminine standard. This was especially true a couple of decades ago, when the ubiquity of big-assed, big-thighed, big-hipped curvature wasn't a regular staple of magazines or internet influencers. Outside of glossy print or pixels, the femme allure of Black women doesn't always expand into their dating prospects. And when it came to small towns in the aughts, the competition was high and the pickings were slim. Both Ashiwa and Dawn came abroad with a not-so-secret hope that seven to ten days might lend them a better chance at love than the seven to ten previous years. Or even just the hope of an ego boost from somebody wanting to flirt with them. I mean, it's intensely boring to recognize you've got a little bit of something cute going on and yet nobody ever looks at you—a full-blown travesty. What everyone had told my women friends about Italian men was that they were intense flirts and seriously into Black women, so they hoped their travel abroad might bring at least a look or two.

I was hiding the fact that I had an Italian boyfriend from my girlfriends. At the time, keeping him a secret seemed better than announcing that I had joined a different club. I hadn't really decided to like myself, and having the people who knew that side of me in the presence of someone who saw me, remarkably, differently, was oddly terrifying. Who knows. I was weird and I didn't know how to deal. I didn't want to ask Marcello the inevitable question of whether or not he had hot gondoliers to hook them up with—the two batting their eyes behind me. We were all church girls; I didn't want to be responsible for anybody else's spring break chastity. My relationship with Marcello was very romantic/sexless. I kept it that way. I was twenty-one, still a virgin, nervous about losing my virginity abroad. As much as it seemed like a space of plausible deniability—oh, God—I was so filled with Southern Christian guilt I couldn't even think about a man without his clothes on without being afraid I couldn't go home. And the gondolier was a gorgeous bodybuilder—I thought about "never going home" often. I blushed when I looked at him. His sweet gaze pulled nearly every petal off of me. Looking back, I might have hurt him telling him I wasn't ready to introduce him to my girlfriends, however briefly. But that's gone—that's that.

For the three to four days that the girls were in Venice, my gut lay on butterflies, expecting at any turn we might run into him accidentally. The overture of his walking around the corner played loud to the terrible movie in my mind in which I ducked and hid from my first Italian love—very unladylike—which is why I was relieved when we three boarded our seats on Alitalia headed to Egypt. I looked at the clouds over Venice, relieved, leaving behind my secret boyfriend and all my potential sins.

In the spirit of my twenties, I didn't waste a minute of time before I suggested we hit the streets of Cairo. We set our suitcases down in the Egyptian Hyatt and headed to the same market where our Bible friends had been a celebrity sighting. Khan el-Khalili, located only a few blocks away from the Nile. We'd been warned to dress modestly, but as church girls from the Bible Belt we took that warning pretty liberally. We spent most of our time, in our world, as pinnacles of feminine virtue. I took to the streets in a midcalf skirt—jersey and bright pink—and long white sleeves. The girls wore jeans, all three of us wore denim jackets and neck scarves. The evening was dark but the weather was warm; I thought I was being as "modest" as possible—but I've never felt more naked than in the twenty minutes my calves were out at Khan el-Khalili bazaar. Like one of those dreams where you're on a playground naked, and everyone notices that you're naked, and everyone decides to say so. I've actually never had that nightmare, I just had that one time I decided to walk with my calves out in Cairo. Silly me.

That's when the paparazzi started. A few moments after we entered the bazaar, men began calling at us to take photographs on their Nokia phones or grabbing our wrists. "Miss, come here, come here." Some of them ordered us to follow them into rooms where we could buy fragrant oils or beautifully embroidered dresses. Others pointed us toward dark alleys to take us somewhere else. None of us wore headscarves. An Egyptian man with an English accent stopped us. He explained that men in the market thought that we were loose women, or Christians.

"But we are Christians," we explained. He shrugged. He pushed away a man who was coming up to us with a digital camera. Ashiwa and Dawn smiled like beauty queens ready to oblige but he yelled at the photographer angrily—"La!"

"Wasn't that rude?" we asked, full of Southern feminine decorum. He understood; he turned to the man and said something more pleasant to soften the blow. Why were we concerned about protecting a man who thought we were loose women? Youth and Stockholm femininity. You tell me. But we walked through the market for a while more, letting a man we'd never met before tell strangers we were either under his care or his kin.

"These men want to take pictures with you so that they can tell people they have slept with you," he told us. My girlfriends got quiet. Loose was one thing, sex was another. The thought

I'd already been thinking sobered them up. Part of what I think our church friends missed in the story of their celebrity was how much the "paparazzi" probably got off seeing a brown-skinned man holding hands with a Midwestern woman. One he was obviously sleeping with. Married or not, it was enough to build out a fetish around in a photograph. A Black woman dating a white man in a foreign country, I thought often about how we looked to everyone else. People looked at my femme and carried all sorts of expectations of me.

●

One night out in Venice, a drunk Fulbright student kept making jokes about my boyfriend while I waited with other students for the night water-bus: asking if I'd been gondo-laid, asking whether or not I had gondorrhea. I threw down my purse and decked him in the face. Such a lady. But in the process of defending my boyfriend's honor, I wondered what he'd told his friends.

I'd started volunteering at a refugee center that was in the same campo I lived in, San Polo. The reality of the fixation Italian men had on black women was as sobering as being photographed at that market. At the refugee camp, several Italian men would lounge around watching TV among the displaced women—some of them girlfriends, some of them women they just hoped to meet. Some of the men would marry them. Some of the women would be pregnant, with half-Italian children who provided them quicker visa status, the babies in their bellies a stronger case for asylum than their original need.

Grabbing croissants at Venice's Rosa Salva café with my boyfriend's black friend, a dreadlocked artist, I made an off-color joke about our skin being a fetish for him. A joke Marcello responded to patiently, but with obvious shock. I never said anything like that to him again. I had to stop assuming I was anything less than someone beautiful he was attracted to. I didn't know how to do that. In order to do that, I had to see myself as someone beautiful to be attracted to. And I had been taught not to value my Black femininity, based on my American upbringing.

•

After the market, the girls and I ran back to the hotel and took business cards for tour guides from the concierge. We threw open our suitcases and searched for every piece of cloth we could cover our bodies with. The clothing hunt became a game. We pulled on our long pants and long sleeves, and put our skirts over them. I draped my jeans and long sleeves in several pashminas.

"This is the way I'm going out from now on!" I proclaimed. I completed the look with a headscarf, adjusting it, liking it a bit. The look was elegant. It gave me a break from the out-loudness of my Afro. I encouraged the girls to do the same but they decided they liked the attention they got with their hair exposed. Ashiwa's dark hair was coiled into thick twists that she accentuated by wearing large hoop earrings, and Dawn, who'd grown out her relaxer for the first time, had soft loose curls that framed her face. They were both pretty girls. It was a shame it took coming into a country in which they were considered loose for them to feel it.

The next night we went out, they would knowingly stop and pose for pictures, sticking a hip out, saying "cheese," and laying into the full breadth of their sensuality. It was our second night in Cairo. We'd scheduled a Nile River dinner cruise that included a theater set of four whirling dervishes and a belly dancer. We weren't the only tourists but all of the other attendees were men. I was covering my hair and kept pulling pashminas out of my messenger bag, suggesting that the girls do the same. They would drape their heads occasionally but with no full commitment. Where we were from, it was a common joke to say "Wear your head covering" to suggest that a woman had forgotten her place. There was a freedom my girl-friends gleaned from flirting with danger, in the freedom of flirting at all, no matter the feminine consequences. They took the scarves to oblige, but throughout the night, the fabric kept slipping off the crowns of their heads.

The dinner theater confused me. For a place so committed to hiding the virtues of womanhood, the boat cruise entertainment was nothing if not feminine and sexual. The four whirling dervishes, with their effete smiles and flamboyant gestures, reminded me of trans beauties on the ballroom circuit, their faces so groomed and dolled they looked like wax. The dancers would openly flirt with the theater guests; it worried me. I assumed at least one of the businessmen would be homophobic. But instead, the rowdy group were turned on and amused. By the time the belly dancer came out, some of the men were in a full lust hysteria, whooping and catcalling as they threw cloth napkins in the air. The dancer looked to be in her sixties, with a solid waist and eye shadow caked into creases. She wore turquoise. She moved in a blur of grace. One of the men grabbed at the dancer by the tail of her skirt. She clapped her hands—"La"—and looked at him seductively. She showed him her silver wedding ring—"Behave," the gesture read; it caused the men to shut up. When she finished performing, they clapped.

●

For the next four days in Cairo, we hired a driver and tour guide to take us around so that we wouldn't be without the company of men. We debated about it; despite the tour guide being a recommendation from our friends, we wanted to travel freely. Our small experience had taught us, if only superficially, that it wasn't easy to be openly femme and alone in the streets of Egypt. Not unlike what we knew of being openly femme and Black almost anywhere else. In this context, it wasn't color that rendered us "exotic" or "outsider" as much as our comfort with Western standards. We fit so well into the most strict of those standards, we couldn't imagine our views would be considered lenient anywhere else.

I asked the tour guide where women went to socialize. I hoped we'd see somewhere outside the darkness of the theater where the femme communed. He told me: "Egypt women see freedom as the dominion of their homes. At home, my wife is boss, out here . . ." He made a common joke we were used to in the South about the man as the head and the woman as the neck that turns it. The girls could finish the phrase before he did, pantomiming the neck swerve and swinging their index fingers.

"Was that a dead body . . . ?" I asked, spinning my head around as we sped past a few people gathered by an overturned moped. The girls didn't see it; it was.

Over the next few days, the tour guide became uncomfortably casual with us. In the beginning, he was generous and patient, escorting us to a light show in Giza and bringing us Cokes for after our camel ride. But by day three, the three of us sick with a stomach bug, he was ordering us to keep pace with him as he breezed through stores owned by people he was close with. He took us to a restaurant where stone-ground bread came hot and fresh off an open assembly-line system that featured a wood-fired oven, leading all the way back to workers grinding its grain in a small mill. It smelled delicious; he grabbed it in his naked hands and broke it in pieces to scatter between us like dogs.

"Eat! Eat!" he said, before turning around to sniff under his dirty fingernails. He gestured for us to follow him with the back of his hand. I wanted to vomit in the bushes.

On the fourth day, we planned to visit a museum. We told him so, showing him which one using the brochure we'd pulled from the Hyatt lobby.

"Why would you want to go to the museum?" he demanded. "The British have already taken everything that's interesting." He had become less and less concerned with our itinerary. He muttered something to the driver in Arabic. We drove. He dialed a number on his cell phone. He was negotiating with the man on his phone, pointing his finger to give the driver new directions. We passed the museum and headed to a commercial business district.

"Where are we going?" I asked. "We said we wanted to—"

"La!" he said, turning around to shush me with one finger. I'd never! I was about to give him a piece of my mind when my girlfriends shushed me, and started joking, trying to turn things into the inside joke we'd kept running since meeting the man at the market. A very feminine predicament—not wanting to make a scene.

When will we realize this ain't safe for us?

The man we'd considered our tour guide walked us through a very drab business expo.

"COME. COME," he said, gesturing to us. He took us into a room where the only thing on sale was pens.

"Ashiwa. Do you want any pens?" I asked, passive-aggressively. The Last Feminine Power.

"Of course I don't," she responded in kind. The guide walked off as if we were invisible. He hurried to the door and greeted six men who joined him with kisses and hearty hand-shakes. To one of them, he gave a slight bow. The man looked to be in his sixties, his slicked-back silver curls thinning, with a huge belly. His face was not unpleasant, but decidedly old. The guide introduced him to all of us. We tried to be polite but we kept looking into the large collection of strange men. It was like being sweet to defuse a bomb.

"Who the heck is this?" Dawn whispered in my ear as the silver man sat down and the entourage worked to get him tea and bottled water. He asked us if we wanted anything. We said no, and a man produced bottled waters for us on a silver tray.

"Drink. Drink." The unfortunate thing about being South-ern femmes is that we retreat at the coarseness of a command. In order to get us out of there, I needed solidarity. Three paying customers against one misogynist. But the girls' eyes glazed at the sight of all this activity, and I could hear their inner dialogue: *It's fine! Just be NICE.* The more uncomfortable we got, the more gracious we were. The men closed in. The silver-haired man cornered Dawn while the tour guide tried to distract us. It was the first conversation he'd tried to entertain us with in days. The silver man told Dawn to sit down beside him. She obeyed; I kept my ears open.

"How old are you? How many children do you have? Have you ever been married? Does Kentucky have an international airport?" It was clear we weren't here to buy anything. It was clear that we were what the tour guide might sell.

"What are you trying to do with my friend back there?" I asked our guide, interrupting his forced conversation. He gave me a wicked smile.

"Your friend is very attractive, very beautiful, she has a look we really like here, around the face"—he gestured to Dawn's beauty gap—"the body . . . ," he said, gesturing to everything else. "She could marry very well here. You . . . not so much." He snorted at his own humor. I looked to Ashiwa—quiet and eyes wide. I didn't know where we were; I didn't know what to do. Dawn was growing increasingly pale as the heavy-set man drew closer to her. I shook my head and straightened my head covering. I walked over and sat on the expo table in front of them.

"Dawn—do you want to marry this man?" I demanded.

She straightened and stuttered, "Oh! Oh goodness, no," she said, shuffling out of the chair.

"Shut up! Shut up, Scary Spice!" said the tour guide. He worded something of an apology to the silver man as we stormed out the expo, all three of us linked in arms.

●

On the drive back to our hotel, our tour guide and I shouted at each other.

"You're the type of American woman who always wants to be the man!" he spat at me as his final insult. I don't know what I fired back. I thought about how I'd grown up, lank and feisty. I thought about how, as the tallest girl in Bible study, I was always asked to learn the male parts when we took waltz classes or salsa danced.

"Let, me, lead!" a Dominican man once yelled at me, stomping his feet on the dance floor. I didn't want to be a man. I was just too in-between to be bossed around by any gender.

As the man yelled on, a stranger to us whose services we were paying for, I waited for my friends to defend me. Neither of them said anything.

At the end of the drive it was me, again, who continued to haggle with the man as he started to extort the price of our trip. I'd had it. I threw more cash at him than he asked for and slammed the door.

"Scary Spice?" Ashiwa asked. I shrugged. I knew what he meant. She was the loudest, most garish girl he could think of at the moment. The Black woman among the Spice Girls, however unladylike. How very like me.

•

It was our final night in Cairo. Alexandria was in the morning. Defeated, we went to dinner at Chili's and afterward walked along the Nile with me singing the song from the chain's commercial: "I want my baby back, baby back ribs." I was wearing my head covering, my two girlfriends letting their hair catch the river breeze. I wondered how Nefertiti and all the queens of ancient Egypt did it.

Close to the Hyatt, we passed an Egyptian woman around our age, in a cream-colored hijab, on a romantic walk with her man. She gasped and covered his eyes while we walked past, and I'd never felt more feminine.

On Trafficking

Shanghai, China

I used to frequent the rooftop of a Portland, Oregon, hotel. I'd grab a drink from the bar before heading upstairs to chat with the staff. One evening, the maître d' was putting a sign out front that caught my attention, an advertisement for tours of the hotel's underground, advertised as "a glimpse into the Shanghai Tunnels." Never heard of them before. It was intriguing for me to think of a pipeline that stretched all the way from one port town to another, an aquatic Underground Railroad. The image was fictional, but the thought was provocative. I wanted to know more. The maître d' launched straight into a monologue he'd been waiting to tell someone—someone Black, I assume.

"White slavery," he said, "that's the meaning of the phrase 'being shanghaied.'" I'd been in this position before, someone excited to use "slavery" in a way that might shock me. The first time it happened, I was on a university campus and a balding white man in a tie-dyed shirt looked me in the eye, handing me a flyer.

"END SLAVERY," he said. I shook. I took the pamphlet, assuming it was a campaign against human trafficking. Instead, it was a bunch of NSFW images of the incarceration of chickens. A vegan campaign. At least the maître d's story involved people. I braced myself for the worst.

According to the hotel clerk, "being shanghaied" was a common fate in Portland during the 1850s. The tunnels that extended under the basement of the hotel once linked the city's seedy network of brothels and bars. Seamen would port and party, and an unlucky number of them would end up roofied and trafficked into an underground white slave trade, connecting East to West along the surface of the Pacific Ocean. He handed me a brochure. I flipped through it. I googled it. I found an article by a local woman activist suggesting that even though much about the tunnels was urban legend, Portland's large network of strip clubs still used some of its underground Shanghai basements, where children were trafficked from Asia, Central America, and Eastern Europe to work as prostitutes—something the city could do something about, though the brochure never mentioned that.

I forgot about the Shanghai Tunnels until I visited Shanghai myself a year later. It was 2018. The Shanghai skies were a weak pink, postapocalyptic neon. Riding into Shanghai on the Nanpu Bridge, with the city below and the sky wrapping the torso of high-rises, I felt like I'd crossed over into the future. Westworld meets Tomorrowland, an amalgam metropolis we Americans can only dream of. Looking up from the speeding car, I saw high-rises disappear in the smog clouds. But most of the city below the height of the skyline was in tatters. Tenements surrounding a luxurious port city. Not my first taste of disparity, but it shook me. The technologically wealthy and the economically poor. In Shanghai the benefits of money are transparent. Money means more space, better air quality, and the possibility of privacy. Premiums even Americans don't pay. The gap between the 1 percent and the rest of us is a rising elevator, and Shanghai is a trip straight up.

It's an easy city to dream in. The architecture is an international mix of Renaissance, neoclassical, and modern, alongside fantastical contemporary structures. Floating orbs. Twisted glass teeming with expensively suited financiers. Everything looks impossible but nothing is, if that makes any sense.

The Shanghai arts district is in a set of old port warehouses. It's one of the few spaces in the city proper where the buildings are less than four stories tall. I never asked who was funding the art, or how the artists managed to pay for the luxury of space, but looking at the large warehouses with paintings constructed on LCD monitors and other tech interventions, I got the sense being a starving artist in Shanghai just wasn't a thing. The artists were friendly, and willing to take the time to discuss their practice at length, without a hint of the pressure that time was money and I was wasting it. I should mention that the friend of mine who was hosting me was wealthy, an author and local arts benefactress. But because we were both Black and dreadlocked, I wasn't sure how much of the time we garnered was out of curiosity and how much of it was out of recognition for what my host represented to the arts community.

Often, it was an obvious, genuine dialogue. We spent over an hour with an artist whose studio practice centered around a copyrighted reproduction of his face. He painted himself on murals and cast himself onto mugs and large ornaments. Both his face and the space had an incredibly pleasing quality; I love an artist who understands both their good looks and their good taste. My host translated the conversation. She explained he was using the reproduced image as a biographical representation of his experience growing up through the rise of Communism. I bought a mug, but wished I had the space to take home something larger; he gave me his business card and told me to stay in touch.

Something about the story of copying and rewriting made me think about the Shanghai Tunnels again. I'd avoided thinking about them because of my concern that the term "white

slavery" was just liberal white Americans' way to brand themselves as victims, and people of the global majority as perpet-
uators of the same savagery their ancestors enacted upon
anyone they considered less than them. The Shanghai Tunnels were a shell game. A swindle. Especially when there were
still people in Portland for whom slavery was imminent.

The Shanghai Tunnels weren't the first time I'd heard about
sex trafficking in Portland. A colleague of mine who'd lived in
Portland for decades—a private school teacher—had spent
years as a sex work advocate. At one point, she'd unofficially
fostered a Latino teenager who'd been brought to Portland in
a box when he was fifteen. To protect him, she never told me
much more. But personally, what I do remember is how casu-
ally Portlanders would mention underage dancers at nightclubs. On a night out, soon after I'd arrived, a group of new
acquaintances decided to hit up one last club before the night
ended. The strip club only served juice. Very Portland. Except,
when I asked why, one of the locals told me it was because
many of the dancers were too young to drink. This didn't sit
right with me. I went home.

In Shanghai, I hopped on Twitter. A few more stories of
the Shanghai Tunnels had begun to show up in Portland feeds,
confirming the fact the tunnels had never fallen out of use.
Some of the underage dancers and sex workers who populated the city's nightlife during business hours were hidden in
the tunnels' caverns during the day. It was strange. To think

of all those sunny happy hours where I stepped over the threshold of the hotel never thinking who might be beneath. A world of slavery, white, Asian, Latinx, and beyond, still trafficking like blood through veins.

•

Sitting in a rooftop bar above the Shanghai clouds, my host and I were having brunch. A man walked up to us, commenting we were the first Black women he'd had the pleasure of meeting in weeks. It was Barry Jenkins. He sat down before we even invited him to and I took in the scene—our large sunglasses, the table adorned with flutes and fruit—which looked like something he'd directed. He wanted to know how we ended up there and I turned the stage over to my friend, and he listened to her story as if scanning the pages of a screenplay. It was beautiful, watching Blackness traffic in the most unexpected of places. That we, the descendants of slavery, now decide and surprise each other in the ways we show up. We have so far to come, but I hope every generation past enslavement has its stories recorded.

We visited the same rooftop hotel bar one more night before I left Shanghai. Personally this was a less elegant outing. It was the opening to a literary convention largely sponsored by my host's money. She was sick, agitated, but felt obligated to make an appearance. I don't know Shanghai politics. I was sitting on the floor of her Shanghai penthouse playing with her cat while she changed and changed clothes. I knew she had a habit of pushing herself; I suggested we didn't have to go. She took it out on me; we fought. The argument lasted well through the car ride, and so she told the driver to keep circling so we could finish the fray and still make a dignified arrival.

I couldn't help but get lost in the architecture. Somewhere, in a pause for peace, I finally asked the Shanghai benefactress whether or not the stories of "white slavery" were true. She slipped into the role of a historian. Yes. There was definitely truth in it.

"But the way the story is told," she said, "is deeply misleading." As stories of race often are. "The reason why so many white people were trafficked from America to Shanghai during the 1850s was because all the European hotels built to accommodate French and Swedish bankers and diplomats had patrons who had refused to be waited on by a Chinese person. It was impossible to encourage enough poor whites to immigrate to staff them." It wasn't just Americans who were affected. White people of various ethnicities were also drafted into servitude. The whims of the technologically rich weighed against the freedom of the economically poor, and this dynamic continues today.

The tunnels linking the Pacific Far East to the Pacific Northwest might be mythical, but the pipeline of human trafficking is everywhere, paved with money and power, and very

real. We keep attaching a price to what each of us is worth—
in our time, in our talents, in what we are to each other. The
benefactress and I took the elevator into the clouds one more
time and it opened into a gilded celebration. We never said a
word again about the urban legend—or many more to each
other—and slid into the luxurious surroundings as if nothing
were different.

Lisbon, Portugal

Naky's from Togo. He's Claudia Rankine's *Citizen* in the form
of a walking tour book. What I like about this as a comparison
is that both are guides.

When I went to Rankine's reading of *Citizen* in Portland,
several of the city's liberal attendees got angry at her portrayal
of racism in the United States because, in my opinion, they
wanted to think of her as a Black person instead of a black
one. They wanted an author observing the microcosm of ag-
gressions the way an African American would, when in reality she is Jamaican, cataloging the strangeness of my home
country from an observer's stance.

Naky's perspective on Portugal is similar. He came to Lisbon married to a Spaniard. Already an EU citizen. A lover of
science and history, a romantic, a keen observer of the world,
and a bit of a rogue. The objectivity with which Naky tries to
approach Portugal's colonial past, its history of human traf-

ficking, is not the kind of distance most people in the world can keep. We are not often that patient. We want the clarity of a hero and a villain. We want to move on. And Naky does too, but with a clear curiosity about what our moving on means. What stories are told by it. In this way, perhaps, he moves too much on his guided tours. That careful sage that Rankine renders in her tongue, Naky traffics in his body. They are two observational critics with a magnitude of understanding for the spaces they inhabit, and in getting to know Portugal, I greatly appreciated knowing both of them.

Not unlike the time while I was living in Portland where, among my circles, passages quoted from *Citizen* carried a certain currency, throughout my Lisbon travels, I could ascertain whether a person was kindred or not based on how they reacted to the stories I shared from Naky's tour. We could be connected through one collective thought.

What were the stories Naky shared? Well, that's proprietary information. I wouldn't give that much of his gig away. But, what I can tell you is, quite often, we in his tour group would be standing at the same monument as another group that was receiving a very different version of the past. Our group was mostly Black and Brown individuals, with a selection of conscientious allies. We easily recognized, just by the tone adopted by white guides of any nearby tour group, that the "knowing" of history for us carried—for our group and theirs—a very different agenda.

I was in Lisbon teaching in a summer program attached to a few Lisbon cultural institutions. A white male American literature professor of Lisboan ancestry and I were on a trip to a museum, and shared a taxi with an older white woman, a program student. She was a poet and professor. She kept directing the conversation back to "the preservation of Lusophone culture." The longer she talked, the more I inched closer to the doorframe of the speeding car, weighing the odds of how well my body would do if I jumped from the car mid-traffic. When I had told her I was a poet as well, she assumed I must be a student of my white male counterpart. I was tired of people assuming that. I was also genuinely surprised by the lack of interest most of the Lusophone advocates I met on my trip had in Brazilian literature.

"What do you mean?" I asked her, naïvely turning the thought over in my fingers like a key. "Brazilian literature is some of the most renowned in the world. Portuguese is one of the most popular languages in the—" I stopped myself. I'd misunderstood. As an American, I already had my answer. Maybe both of us had missed the fact she was trying to speak in code. Somehow she assumed—from, what, my English, my sense of the academy, that we were briefly traveling partners?— that I would somehow agree with her views about the need for the erasure of dark-skinned people from Lusophone heritage. That that was a world I would understand as correct.

One of the most surprising things for me about arriving in

Lisbon is that I had absolutely no idea how Black the city was when I arrived. I had met a few Portuguese people from my time living in the Netherlands, but I knew very little of their history and culture. Knew so little in fact, despite being a teacher of things myself, that I didn't know that Lisbon was one of the earliest sites of the slave trade—human trafficking being traced to Lisbon as early as the fifteenth century. This was a place that I was ignorant of as a part of my own origins. I had been blissfully stupid, assuming Lisbon's history to be something like the information I imagined the white tour guides routinely dealt out. Something sleepy, and a bit dull, in comparison to the stories of the fiery conquests and historic valor of the Spaniards and the Italians, with some vague mention of music, color, and a distinct modern literary tradition thrown in. I realized, in retrospect, this is how white Americans had always described Portugal to me.

One of the things that kept me so blind to Portugal's importance to the slave trade is that instead the country markets its role in history as that of the more benevolent colonizer. The underdog of western European colonization. The kindly bottom-feeders of the commonwealth. Of course, I wasn't ignorant of the idea that Brazilians and Angolans didn't cross the seas to teach themselves Portuguese, but I had never questioned what those trading routes had looked like. That it was the Portuguese, for instance, who'd determined the shortest route between Africa and the New World, a fact I doubt they ever sing about in their fado music. No matter how close I might feel to the historical victimhood in Portugal's humble, emotional European origin story, the Portuguese are not the "Black people" of Europe. Black people still are. And the Portuguese still participate—actively and systematically—in our erasure.

Portugal today is a country that considers itself race-blind and uses no terms to distinguish between its Black and white citizens, because the only language they have is discriminatory. Although this was hard for me to believe, the story was later corroborated by a white English expatriate, a woman who worked in advertising, semiotics. When she first moved to Lisbon, her boyfriend—who'd been born there—was Indian by ethnicity and raised in Mozambique. At a party with a bunch of liberal Lisbon intellectuals, she ventured to ask what they would call an African from Mozambique, or any Black person by extension. After a lot of conversation, the crew, the equivalent of the Lisbon literati, decided there was no way to address a Black person in Portuguese. The only words that existed, "preto" and "negro," were racial slurs. "The best way to address race in Portuguese is to not say anything," one of the party attendees explained to her. But this "blindness" covers over the immutable truth that Black people—their cultural contributions, their very existence—are a huge part of the history of the Portuguese that the Lusophone world refuses to acknowledge. And as terrifying as that is to consider, it helps me understand how I could fly all the way overseas and know so little about a country that had affected my origins so much.

On the tour, Naky had introduced us to shops owned by people across the diaspora. Aside from the African shop owned by Guineans, we'd passed shops owned by Angolans, Ghanaians, and Congolese—not to mention Afro-Brazilians.

"Despite this broad presence of people of African descent across the Continent, how do the Portuguese continue to deny Black people in their data?" I asked, adopting my most professorial tone to thinly disguise a question cut out of pure rage. He sighed and described his early days looking for hubs in which Africans networked as groups instead of ethnic factions. They didn't exist. People socialized similarly to how the census represented them, Black people mostly mixing only within groups of their countries of origin, despite some of those same Black people being able to trace their roots in Portugal back to the first slave ships. As a Black person, there is no standardized way to claim Portugal as your own. According to the Portuguese, there are no Black-Portuguese people, no Black-Portuguese culture, no existence of Black culture in the hyphenate.

This fact itself is what made African-Lisboan tour groups like Naky's such an essential part of international Black travel. The thing to get hip to within Naky's tour was that the tour itself was a network, a sort of food, a place of refuge where the diaspora announced themselves and smuggled information. What we learned on the tour mattered, but it didn't matter nearly as much as the annotations that emerged as side comments by Nigerian lawyers and psychologists, South Carolinian filmmakers, the folks from around the globe who added their own notes to the tour's abundant knowledge. The tour was not just a study of Lisbon's history, but a compendium of all of us whose bodies had been bought, sold, and exploited in some way by the Middle Passage.

For example, I briefly dated a man from Togo who told me that while the rest of West Africa was selling other tribes to early slave ships (some on their way to Lisbon, historically), the people of Togo had been conscientious objectors of a sort. Sorted against the sordid affair of selling humans. I asked Naky if what his fellow countryman had told me was true, and he thumbed through his things to show me an early map of the West African coast. He pointed out that it would have been impossible to separate Togo from Ghana, or Nigeria, or any other context, since all of those colonial labels were newly applied. This is what I mean about Naky's objectiveness; I thanked him for this. I enjoyed the clarity of the way he went about my education. I thought back to the American English professor with whom I shared the car ride, the programming she was trying to trade as something other than racist, whereas in Naky's tutelage, he did not even exempt his own people.

According to Naky's narrative, no one in the history of human trafficking was the colonial underdog, except the trafficked.

•

On a walk with the Englishwoman, the semiotics expert, she told me about the novel she'd been writing, and I asked her about what had been her favorite part of living in Lisbon during the pandemic.

"The walks," she said. Exploring a new city that was basically hers and her then-beloved's. But even in celebration of something so simple as how we enjoyed our time when the world was still, it was still hard not to come back to the strange erasure of Black history in Portuguese culture. She mentioned that, on one of her first walks, her local Mozambican boyfriend pointed to a street whose name roughly translated to "the Well of Blacks" in English. Her boyfriend had shared the same story Naky's tour group had shared with me; the street was named as such because an immense number of Black people had been buried there, thrown into a ditch the length of a city block, after they had all been promised—in exchange for their conversion—decent Christian burials. The bodies were stoned over. And above it were built the houses where most early free Black people lived. Today, the street is gentrified—idyllic—and it is only its second history, its softer past, that the Portuguese choose to commemorate. The Englishwoman said a white Portuguese man she was on a date with corrected her when she suggested that "well" was a euphemism, insisting this street was called "the Well of Blacks" simply because, in its heyday, "the-people-we-do-not-name" would have been teeming out of its jazzy seams. I imagined Black people hanging out the windows of the Well singing fado.

"The truth is so obvious," one of us had said. I can't remember which.

On that part of the tour, Naky had studiously produced a letter from a Portuguese king listing the street clearly as an African mass grave. He showed us pictures of a contemporary archaeological dig in which the bodies of those people had been excavated in contorted positions, with their hands and feet bound. He further supported the evidence that they were African with some historical facts about dentistry records: West Africans were known throughout colonial Europe as coming from the coast with the healthiest teeth, since dentistry was a common practice throughout parts of the Continent. The "truth" was so obvious. But truth, after truth, after truth, after truth . . . It was so shocking. There were moments when hearing the history of Lisbon that I felt parts of myself die with each tragedy. I was happy that we built a community of friendship and allyship walking beside Naky because, in truth, I needed that support in order not to dwell on the trauma.

———

Throughout my weeks in Lisbon, Naky and I would randomly intersect as I explored more historically Black venues, and he toured larger and larger groups of tourists through those restaurants and nightclubs. People were coming from all over the world by word of mouth, Instagram, and Airbnb. He'd become a bit of an urban legend among Black expats. One night while I sat with one of Naky's night tours, finishing off sugary cocktails at a bar called Brooklyn, Naky got a strange direct message. A burner Instagram account cursing him out for his reportage on a statue of a revered Lisbon priest.

A plaque accompanied the statue, reading roughly in English, "Padre António Vieira S.J.: Political Diplomat, Defender of Indigenous Human Rights." But etched beside the official text, in bloody, faded spray paint, were the words: "Day of Portugal, Day of Racism," a monument to the moment in 1996 when neo-Nazis stormed Lisbon, killing at least ten African residents before they were stopped. The harasser on the burner account tried to claim this event never happened, calling Naky a terrorist and threatening to kill Naky himself. It was hard to watch a man who only wanted to tell the truth receive a threat to his life. We all tried to shake it off but after it, the evening felt ruined. Many of us dispersed—and that was the point.

For years, countries like Portugal have loved to publish information about colonization and gentrification as signs of progress. What no one seems to be tracking, other than tour guides like Naky, is an African expatriate renaissance. A "renaissance" in the spirit of Harlem legends like Baldwin, Baker, and Hughes taking to Paris for self-actualization, except the call to freedom isn't singular, it's many. African-Lisboan tours are just the beginning. Within these tours people can find access to an entire network of Black people from around the world who are moving to Lisbon in droves because the cost of living is affordable, the weather is pleasant, and it's not difficult to build camaraderie among like-minded people of color. Black people in particular seem to be finding adventure in Lisbon as a worthy destination on its own or as part of any nearby travel itinerary.

I didn't know this. I don't know who's telling everybody how lit it is. But it's like the best-kept/worst-kept secret: that the same country that began the great forced migration of Africans all over the world is now becoming the place where its young intellectuals gather freely. I would have never guessed. But I imagine that the fact that this feeling is palpable—a sea change—is the reason why the white Portuguese take this shift in Lusophone culture as such a threat.

The traffic in Lisbon is history-making right now and we'd all do well to put our ear to it. Just think: the city that created the African diaspora is now the hub for calling us all back together. As an American, I never imagined an era in which the countries that pulled us apart would be the places where we did our best repair work—on our own, through global grass-roots activism on European soil—but this was the great gift of Lisbon for me. It changed everything.

For the first time, the African diaspora has an accessible urban hub where we can disseminate ideas among each other; disseminate among each other the knowledge we need to re-build. And, as African Americans, we don't have to watch Pan-African growth happen from places on the Continent that are too difficult for most of us in the middle class to af-ford in a lifetime. We finally have a focal point; that's some-thing I'm proud of. If we want to, in Lisbon, the Pan-Africans can party, love, and get cute—because, hell yes, we love all that shit—but we can also shift ideas about what Black cul-ture means to the world. I see African Lisbon tours as a new Freedom Train, the aggregators, the internet's new Blackness, with people like Naky as its traffic conductors.

On my last night in Lisbon, accompanied by dozens of members of the tour group and Lisbon's Black young expatri-ate population, I danced around with more countries than I'd ever seen in one club. We gathered in a circle, charmed by our makeshift ambassadorship, and repped our countries with our dance moves. Mali and Senegal and Eritrea. Nigeria, Soma-lia, Ghana, Kenya, and Madagascar. Brazil. The United States: Washington, DC; Pennsylvania; New York; Los Angeles; Ken-tucky.

I stumbled into a corner to catch my breath with Samah,

an oil executive, my new Eritrean friend. She'd recently moved from London to Lisbon and had just made the migration permanent. She said the cutest thing I've ever heard about being a usurper.

"The colonizers are dead," claimed Samah. "I am the colonizer now. I won't eat their food. I won't learn their language. I make more money than them. And I am staying here. We are moving here and we are going to take this all back." We went back to the dance floor, ending the night in a reverie of our brown skin swirled in the haze of hookah smoke and purple strobe lights.

Lisbon is a well of Blackness come alive. A river reclaiming the traffic lost.

And yes, we will get it all back.

On Love

New York, New York

"I love New York." The first time I ever said this, I was coming out of a subway stop for the 4 5 6 at Grand Central Terminal. It was hot—October—and I was headed to a tiny fellowship, at an even smaller desk, at the Fifth Avenue New York Public Library, the one with the lions out front. Despite its being my second time living in the city, up until then I'd still only thought of it through the lens of my early childhood memories of *The Wiz* and *Sesame Street*.

I said "I love New York," noiselessly, under my breath, frequently in that first year of my return to the city. The words felt as good as a first crush. I was lonely and missing someone. The hole in my heart felt big enough to stick my whole hand through it. I had friends in the city, wonderful ones, but I felt constantly aware of what I could be doing in New York—

partying, looking fabulous, rubbing elbows with celebrities; every moment covered in other people's glitter—versus what I was actually doing: going out occasionally, mostly to rooftops, cute dinners, the opera, or experimental theater. This awareness filled me with fear that it was my boringness, my solitude, that made me not enough for him.

He only lived in Brooklyn. And we'd rendezvoused, pretty adorably, for several months while I was back and forth between Portland and Manhattan, until I got a job that brought me back to East Coast living, at which point he stopped returning my messages. That had been spring. By summer we ran into each other on the platform of a broke-down A C subway line on Fulton where they'd made us all exit the train and wait for a new one, when I was scrambling to make it to a Hinge date. I was standing on the platform trying to get two bars of cell service. The train came in, and his train car opened. For a brief moment he stood there, looking at me like he loved me, so, of course, I said something dumb.

"It's Shayla," I said, snapping my fingers to say, *Snap out of it.* In truth, the way he ghosted me—the way being left on read by him haunted me, lived with me—made me truly worried that he had forgotten my name. He looked me up and down. I realized he thought I looked pretty. We'd dated in fall and winter. He'd never seen me summer-dressed. He walked onto the platform. We flirted and made small talk about the book he was reading on cryptocurrency. I pulled the book out of his hands.

"You know I write these, don't you?" Of course he did. In fact, he'd come to my last book's debut poetry reading in DUMBO when we were still . . . canoodling. I'd texted him, telling him to bring his wildest friend, and he did—his wildest friend and my wildest friend, and then the two of us went out for cocktails afterward. That night, on his couch, after we spooned for two hours watching a screening edit of an upcoming android film, I kissed his softly snoring mouth. He woke to me kissing his hairy belly—which I loved, maybe considerably, more than him. And he asked if we could keep our relationship more casual.

I thumbed through the book on the train platform. He looked at me, puzzled.

"Where are you headed?" he asked. The train conductors were trying to screech the engine back to life. I hemmed and hawed. I wanted to be coy but my heart beat too fast beside him to lie. He'd moved his messenger bag and was so close in front of me, our light jackets touched.

"Out. To meet . . . a friend . . . I'm headed to . . . dinner(?)."

He smiled. Just as coy as I couldn't be. He kissed me and the train whirred back to life, catching my dress in the wind of its engine. He held his arms around my waist.

"Have fun!" he said, hopping back on the train before it beat on. And—of course—I absolutely could not.

By October, I wasn't missing him as much as I was missing that I could be loved by him, and wasn't. And that it was only by virtue of something I was that I wasn't. I didn't know what "was" was, but I knew I felt it often now in New York.

I had the people I loved who loved me, but I was doing a terrible job at enamoring anyone new. For friendship or otherwise. I'd have weird short dalliances and meet interesting people at bars, us each promising to call each other afterward, but that was something we'd never do. "You're very West Coast," people would tell me often, which was funny to me because I rarely told people I'd moved from Portland, Oregon, and I had only lived there three years. I'd given up heels for Jordans. Was that the tell? I think what they were referring to was my pie-eyed openness, my excitement for new encounters. Everyone I met moving back to the city was distrustful of my eagerness.

But I've always been like that.

When I lived in New York the first time, in my mid to late twenties, I used to run around town in this "I ♥ KY" T-shirt. I wore it ironically but just happened to have that sentiment in spades. In one of my favorite pictures of me from 2008, I'm at a Harlem house party and pausing for a moment from dancing the floorboards down in a prewar apartment—to "Nasty Girl" by Vanity 6 and "Hypnotize" by Biggie—when the neighbors downstairs knock a broomstick against their ceiling in the break while we are switching tracks to tell us to keep it down. I'm wearing big, square, purple glasses. They've completely fogged up. And in the moment when my friend snaps a picture of me in the half-blown-out flash of an actual digital camera, my shirt's twisted in a way where the "K" in my confessional T-shirt looks like an "N."

It's hard to say if I loved New York when I was young. I was living there but still trying to find my way. Kentucky had raised me but hadn't particularly loved me much. "You're not from here," bluegrass strangers would say to me all the time when I was out in my hometown. "You look like you're from New York." And so I moved there, because it was the place where I "lived."

No matter how New York I looked, Kentucky was what I was. And I was so green and gullible that the story all my Harlem friends told to introduce me was from the time a wild-looking man in a trench coat, standing beside the West Fourth Street basketball courts downtown, had very forcibly tried to sell me a rolled paper sack filled with white Gap cotton thongs. Underwear. And it wasn't the fact it happened that made them laugh. It was the fact that I seemed to them the most likely sucker to buy a bag of something I didn't want from a pushy man in the streets to "just be nice."

"Kentucky!" That was the nickname one of my new friends from the Bronx gave me. I loved it. I kept hoping her nickname would stick. It seemed to upend the uneasiness I felt about how guileless I was at every turn, in a city that needed beguiling.

"You can be nice, sweetie," said one of the old church ladies I'd go sit beside on the park benches at 120th and

Morningside—who were always in Sunday hats and stockings—because they reminded me so much of the women I knew from home. "You can be nice, sweetie . . . but not too nice." Or "not that nice," she may have said. The tales of my naïveté were unbecoming, even to her.

But for me, New York was neither an un-becoming or an undoing. The ways in which I wasn't whom she, the City, wanted (the ways in which I wasn't whom he wanted) taught me so much about being in love.

Love is different from being in love. I'm an abundant over-lover, but being in love is something I was bad at. I've moved around so many times. And I've lost so many people. I just want some constancy and certainty. I can't stand the catch and release. And falling in love with New York is a very particular type of unrequited love. She is grimy and overstretched but beautiful and powerful. And the kind of people people like to fall in love with in New York share that dichotomy of vision and dysfunction. Like, I knew the minute I'd met the kind of woman the train platform man could be with, at the after-party to a winter party. She was five foot two and energetic. She had an impressive but uninteresting job. She'd recently been broken up with and had just moved into a single-girl studio. But the confidence she projected over plastic-cup cocktails. Enviable.

Impeccable. I listened to her talk for probably a half an hour. About how quickly she would find another boyfriend, and how happy she was to be on to the next. She was pretty, but not leaning in either direction where I'd add an adjective to it. In short, she was no more extraordinary than I could have been, to the right imagination. But in her power of projecting past her circumstances, past all the insecurity that is possible, she was a force of sheer will. What she knew that I refuse to learn is that falling in love is about building a mythology around who you really are. Falling in love is a surface.

"Don't you worry about starting over?" I asked her, fascinated. I'd started over far more times, but I was excited to hear what a girl I couldn't be might say. She shrugged, unruffled.

"The boys will take care of me," she said, gesturing around the crowded bar to the boy I was in love with and his friends. "They've already been so great to me." She said that part so honestly, so sweetly. In calling "in love" a surface, I'm not saying it lacks any real charm or honesty; each surface has its own texture, depth, and quality. But, at some point, this wears off.

I envision this as the reason so many people I meet in New York describe relationships as a process of falling in love, only to realize that the person they fell for isn't the same as the person they dated. I don't feel pity for these people, even under the best of circumstances. Theirs is a completely unreasonable expectation. But I think New Yorkers are more prone to expect a person they love will maintain the pretense of being in-love-able much longer than anywhere else because that person has the City—sexy, unyielding, and confident—to compete with.

You know the fantasy of the wide-mouth girl who gets dropped off the bus from Anytown onto Forty-Second Street with two bucks and one bag? That's the level of earnestness that's always in me. But at some point, a newcomer is supposed to harden, sharpen, and calcify into a heart stiff enough to game the system. Ten years in and on a second go at the Big Apple, I was supposed to have been the New York girl who, like New York, made you work hard for a sliver of affection. But instead, I still baked pies and left them on lovers' doorsteps. I still always remembered a past love's birthday, and sent goofy GIFs.

I had a great job, an amazing apartment, a new book I was writing, and a fellowship at the Library with the Lions, which made me feel very special. And yet, every person I tried to fall in love with in New York was incapable of loving me back.

I didn't move out of New York because I stopped loving her. I moved out of New York because the thing people don't advertise is that there always comes a time in those New York relationships where the choice is either your life or theirs. And you know, no matter what, they will keep going, that there will always be someone who needs beguiling, even if you're not it.

During the fall of 2020, at the height of a pandemic year where my penchant for care in the form of pies left on doorsteps and goofy text messages made me a bit of a community asset, I started to lose my legs. My right, or left, knee would dislocate without warning. And though this was manageable in a New York world where no one was walking much, I knew by November that New York, in all her masked vulnerabilities, couldn't handle my growing ones. November was the first and last time I felt brave enough to navigate the New York subways by myself, during COVID-19, on my unreliable appendages. I winced at every flight of subway stairs I'd stomped up easily in 2008—often skipping to work back then, or out afterward, in my one pair of clearanced Century 21 Jimmy Choos. I struggled to find the signs that pointed to accessible access points for train cars, the elevators, only to realize that walk was often twice as long as the stairs were up. I had to rest and hold on to things. Because I don't look physically impaired but was obviously struggling, in the COVID-19 era no less, a few people stared at me. The staring, a New York first. One of the best things about the city had always been how much it cultivated anonymity in density, like a loud house party. I found the subway elevator. I entered it.

"Excuse me, miss, this woman needs help." It was a Dominican gentleman who was guiding an older woman who spoke no English to the closing doors. She was a stranger to both him and me. (That's another thing that in New York feels like a beautiful party, the occasional bouts of complete, unselfish kindness from total strangers.) She was trying to get up the stairs, as I was, but as soon as we stepped on the platform she realized the train she needed was in the opposite direction.

"Help me," she said. Strong but diminutive.

I winced. But I did. Walked her back to the elevator, which we took down, and walked a train's length to the next elevator, which put her in the right direction and put me totally off my path. I was tired and in so much pain. I can't even remember if I made it to my neurology appointment, to check if what was going on with my legs was a product of my brain malfunctioning. I must've.

"I love New York." I love New York, but unless you're equipped with an abundant amount of wealth, status, or physical ability, it is an almost untenable city. Because, so often, she does not contribute to those wells of health you are trying to build in order to maintain a relationship with her. Instead, she only takes them. I've dated dysfunctional people. I've dated people who've dated dysfunctional people. And in every version of the tales we tell of being in those loves, I hear, "but, I love her." There is a certain intoxication that comes with falling in love with someone—a person, a city—that has all of the enchantment in the world but absolutely none of its home training. We feel emboldened by the fact that we persevere. It makes us feel we're better than the people who have loved and left. It means we are better, stronger, more ordained. But the one thing being loved and being in love hold in common is that both require reciprocity in their truth. Although it never feels all right to say this amid metropolitan circles, New York—in all her glamour and culture, all her poverty and corruption—is too narcissistic to love any of us back.

I love how Alison Bechdel puts it. "Narcissism is a wound." Because I think of the myth of Narcissus and how he was so consumed with the wound of his self-obsession he could not see that the beauty reflected back at him from a pool of water was entirely his own. I think this is what New Yorkers miss. That when we say "I love New York," we operate from that lofty feeling that she has given us beauty, given us meaning. When it is our own creativity, our own resilience, our own perseverance and patience, that keep her alive in the first place. Before Narcissus was "a wound," he was a flower. A daffodil. A symbol of birth and new beginnings. When I first moved to the city in 2008, what shocked me the most was the number of people who wore the city's toll like a badge, honoring the siege that "New York Shitty" had wrought upon them. Homelessness. Debt. Bad lungs from the poor air quality. Fallen arches from the strain pretty or improper shoes put on our feet. That's the "in love" part. An enamoration that leads to acceptance of the stagnant brutality that surrounds us. Resigned to what we cannot change, we carry the torch of her mythology. When we are her whole story. The *idea* of New York is that if we can't look past what doesn't work for us about her, we'll be shit out of luck finding happiness anywhere else.

But the reality is we are always starting over. Even here, in

spite of her, with her, because of her—us bright, shining or-
ganisms—we are the beauty in her adornment. No matter
who we are or what we become. We who constantly evolve
with this world are her one true romance.

I first moved to Harlem because in my first studio apartment
(in a DUMBO that wasn't DUMBO yet), my landlord had
been stalking me. He lived in the apartment right beside mine
in a co-op where he'd bought two units. Things were fine at
first but, within the first couple months, objects kept "breaking" in my apartment—the air conditioner, the refrigerator,
and once a vase of mine that had been a present—that he kept
claiming he needed to go in and clean up or "fix" while I wasn't
home. He'd always call me after to detail the emergency, which
I told him wasn't right, but he kept doing this anyway. I had no
way to prevent him from entering without changing the locks.

One day, I came back from my job near Manhattan's Flower
District, at an architecture firm across the street from FIT's
campus, to find he'd replaced the meager furniture I had with
leather furniture he claimed to have gotten a really good deal
on, one he couldn't pass up. When I told him this was a violation of safety, moreover, my property, he teared up, asking
why I didn't "appreciate the gift." The older New Yorkers I
knew in Brooklyn Heights balked at me for letting things get
this far. They'd say things like: "You should've worn an engage-

ment ring" or "You should've pretended to have a boyfriend so he'd know to leave you alone." I was fucking twenty-four. Although this should apply for people of absolutely any age, I was old enough to assert my right to safety and freedom without the specter of a man's protection. I called the NYC Housing Authority, I called a lawyer, I called the building's co-op board. The tone in each of their responses was exactly the same. "You could try and fight this but . . . good luck." By that point, I'd spent a few days scrambling to figure out another housing situation and wouldn't return to my studio without having a guy escort me—one of my few friends who'd also migrated to the city or one of the new friends I'd met. It was embarrassing to have them sit around until dark, to at least try to give my landlord the impression that whoever was visiting was staying the night. One of my friends who worked in IT suggested I buy a frequency scanner at RadioShack to check for hidden cameras in the apartment. That felt like more spy shit than I was into, but I did it anyway, expecting nothing to come of it. But it beeped when I took it into my bedroom, when I scanned the closet. I threw it back in the box and took it back.

By day five after the furniture swap, over the weekend, I'd packed what remained of my stuff in black garbage bags and Duane Reade boxes and I moved out. I'd found an apartment on Sublet.com where two women who'd been roommates for years were stuck in a two-person lease they couldn't get out of, even though one of the women needed to move out of the city to attend to a dying family member. I'd brought most of my things to the apartment by myself, with two friends of mine from Harlem, in a U-Haul we had to navigate through the tiny streets of Fort Greene. It had been my dream neighborhood; I thought this quick-turn sublet had God's blessing. The girls asked if we could sit down on the couch to discuss house rules, and my Harlem girlfriend Diana sat beside me. Our other friend made himself busy, shuffling the mattress I'd just bought through the front door. We four girls, all Black women, sat down. Most of the "house rules" were espoused in a very aggressive tone by the roommate who was leaving. At a certain point in the conversation, I said, "This is all good, but I'd much rather hear from the roommate I'll be living with." That clicked off something. The roommate I was supposed to live with got up out of her chair, yelling, ready to fight me.

"Okay!" I said, and slapped my hands on my thighs. "Time for us to go." My friend Thaddeus had just managed to get the mattress through the doorway. The three of us pushed the mattress back into the U-Haul, grabbed my garbage bags, and left.

We didn't know where we were going. I had no place to live. Unbeknownst to me, Thaddeus and Diana had started texting around to the friends they knew uptown to see if I could crash on someone's couch for a while. Diana had four roommates. Thaddeus studied at Columbia and was living in the dorms. They connected me to a friend of theirs, in her early thirties, Chiara, who worked in the Black hair care division at L'Oréal, and was the only person in our collective contact lists who could afford an apartment with a spacious living room and a pull-out sofa. And what was supposed to be a single overnight visit became where I lived for the next six months. Thank god, Chiara and I became friends.

●

"The problem is that underneath all of this 'nice' ... ," I started to say to the church lady I sat beside on the benches lining Morningside Heights about three months into couch surfing in Harlem. As I spoke, I drew large circles around my heart-chest. "The problem is that underneath all this 'nice,' there is just even more 'nice'!" I mean, I was partially joking. But I was pushing against the expectation of how New Yorkers perceived me. In order to survive New York, I was meant to create a fa-çade, a surface, that exalted me to becoming "in-love-able." I didn't want to do that. I have always wanted, more than anything, to be deeply, vastly known. There is a world that says you're not allowed to do that. That perception is every-thing. But even in my early twenties, I prided myself on my authenticity. My candor. I was a small-town artist who really had no big-city dreams. A girl who just wanted to live some-where she could be understood, not presumed to be a certain way because of a stereotype of where natural-haired Black women artists are supposed to reside. By the time I'd moved to New York City, I'd already successfully lived on my own in Italy. I wasn't "green." I chose the path of openness and naïveté because I was curious. That's the only real way to stay in love, I believe. To stay curious enough that opening each part of your heart feels like delicately unhinging each clove from a bulb of garlic, each experience made roughly of the same material but each reflection filled with new reverence. An adventure.

●

Arriving out of the green 4 5 6 subway tunnel in 2018 on my way to the Fifth Avenue New York Public Library, the wind caught my immaculate, oversized autumn coat-sweater, and I felt like perhaps this time New York was radiating a bit of her light on me. I had a stranger snap a photo for Instagram. A lone woman traveler like me. I held on to the leg of one of the lions, lifting one sneaker up as if, Mary Poppins–style, I was about to umbrella away. I posted it on Instagram, hoping that he'd like it. Instead, the comments came pouring in from all over the world from friends of mine about how good returning to the city looked on me. Including one from Marseilles, France, from a deep—possibly lifelong—love of mine: "Oh my God, my dearest. You look so handsome." Although I know I took many more, that's the last picture of myself in the city, of love, that I really remember.

I didn't move out of New York because I stopped loving her. I moved out of New York because the thing people don't advertise about what the city does is that there always comes a time in courting her when you have to decide between your life and hers. Lifetime New Yorkers sacrifice themselves to the adoration of her—her hells and high waters—but I couldn't. Years after I left New York, I read in *Time* magazine that, in the post-pandemic era, 60 percent of America's population has been diagnosed as chronically ill. That includes 60 percent of New York's eight and a half million people, the disabled of New York City alone constituting 4 percent of America's overall population. When I remember us hobbling into the subway desperately searching for elevators, being shoved and called "bitch"—or other names—for moving slower than the rest of the city's microorganism, I understand why I felt, for so long, so unlovable. It wasn't just who I was. It was what I represented in all of us, the admission that imperfection is real. That being impervious to my fragile body is impossible, unnecessary, unhealthy. Because, no matter what, New York will keep loving without me. There will always be someone who needs her beguiling.

What happened to the boy, you ask? I'm so glad you did. Regretfully, I walked carrying around that heart-shaped hole in my heart for at least another year, plugging it occasionally with my fist or other people's kisses. We ran into each other. In Mexico City. A few days before New Year's. I'd taken myself there on a solo trip I'd planned because I wanted to spend the first day of 2020 somewhere entirely new. I'd known he was going to be there, because we'd spent two sweet, unforgettable, but completely drunken days together right before he left, where we ran through the city in the dark from spot to spot, the way I had loved to do with my young friends back in Harlem. I hinted to him I'd be there. I'd booked my ticket and hotel a month before I knew his plan and thought perhaps this was kismet. But when he didn't take the bait, I moved on, assuming there was no way I'd run into him in the largest city in North America, when I barely ran into him living a few blocks away in the second largest.

I was wrong. The first spot I'd booked for my first night out alone was a speakeasy you entered through a Coke machine. He was there.

"Isn't this incredible, us running into each other here?" I said to him and his friend—never smooth.

"Eh," said his Serbian-Brooklyn buddy, "only in New York." The boy looked excited to meet me, but also nervous. The two of them were on a double date with two women they'd met the night before. I'll skip the details, but I ended up tagging along—a fifth wheel. By the end of the night, the Serbian and his date had a fight, and she left, and I decided I too should make my exit. But the girl on the date with the man I was in love with insisted I stay. I got it. She'd just met them. And I was trying not to let on to her what he meant to me (although I'd just mailed him a letter to tell him, at the tail end of that sweater-and-library October, two months ago). Although he kept interrupting the conversation between us two girls to tell her in slurred words I was one of his "favorite people."

We walked a couple blocks or so from our second bar to the Airbnb the boys were renting, and I tried to catch an Uber. But the girl laced her arm in mine, insisting that I cancel it. "This block's not safe. This building's not safe." She went through an itinerary of reasons why neither of us should be there, from murders to earthquakes, but she held on to me too tightly for me to leave, and obviously had plans of staying.

The apartment was beautiful, completely renovated and gentrified. She eased up, and took a seat on the sofa while the Boy brought us beers and his friend disappeared up the spiral staircase, to get to sleeping. The three of us were alone. It was awkward as hell. But the writer in me had kicked in at that point: How often do you get a front-row seat to see the person you're in love with put the moves that worked on you on somebody else? (There are still so many ways I could write this.)

He took the two of us outside to take a look at the view. The whole skyscape of CDMX lit up like New York City. The Girl was wearing a black spaghetti-strap dress and it was too cold for her to stand outside long. He lit a cigarette, and I stood beside him, wrapped in my fabulous October sweater.

"So...," the Boy said. We talked. I only committed the last line he said to memory; even my therapist, years later, would remark that it sounded so terribly earnest. "... I'm just afraid I'm going to go back in there and disappoint her." And in that moment, I knew what I was to do.

As in, I knew what I was meant to do. I recalled the pretty woman I'd met at his after-party. I thought of how, tiny town that she was, she towered over me by the sheer metropolis of will in her presence. I was supposed to be that. I was supposed to walk off the porch and into the living room and tell that girl this night was no longer hers and he belonged to me. If I had, I sometimes think, maybe we'd be together right now. Maybe we'd be buying each other plants and cozying up on his couch, and I'd never write these words because we'd be too busy making love to each other. And I finally would have become a New York girl. But I didn't want to.

"Your date got all dressed up to be here with you," I said, "and we shouldn't keep her waiting." We walked back indoors, where she was flushing the toilet and returning to sit down on the sofa. She took out a small bag of cocaine and the two of them started snorting it, off the back of a key, while queuing up YouTube videos of Lauryn Hill on her iPhone. I could now discreetly exit, but I didn't do that either. I asked the Boy to walk me out. He was trying to finish our conversation as he escorted me downstairs—saying how proud he was of all he'd seen me do since we'd met and how I was about to blow up, like so many of the friends he'd made in New York over the years. But the tears in the back of my eyes were burning too fast for me to turn around, or let him catch up, and this is why I consider myself an un-"in-love-able" girl, because stopping the hurt is the only time I'm built to put a façade up. By the time we'd walked the four flights down to my Uber, I was composed and cool, all the parts of me that loved him suffocating in the car's trunk.

I told him to hit me up when his trip was over, which he never did, and with the pandemic starting soon after the New Year began, I never saw him again.

He wrapped himself around me in that way that made me mush, both his arms at the base of my waist, like that day on the C train. But this time he didn't let go as he did when he heard the ding of the moving subway train. He kissed me, and I tried to pull away—I tried thinking about what he would soon do with that same mouth—but I slid into it. Then I pulled the handle of the car door open just quick enough so that I didn't slide myself right back into trouble.

"This is one of my most favorite girls in the world," he told the cabdriver in inebriated American Spanish. "Be careful with her or you answer to me," he said. I rolled my eyes. But, before I stepped into the car he hugged me one last time, and said to me the only thing I'd been waiting for New York to say to me after so many years: "I love you." Best thing in the world he ever did for me was that he didn't.

On Time

A woman that I love more than life once told me, "Disability is really just a measure of time." With time, all of us will be different than we are right now. In sickness, we all become time travelers. "Disability is just time working differently on the body." At a certain point in time, we all will have to consider what we can no longer do. Some of us just reconcile with this earlier.

Frida Kahlo's house is cobalt blue. Entering the organism, I'm reminded of how color has been a constant companion in the midst of a life filled with so much pain. Color so lush I can taste it, my tongue softly drowning in color. In her pain, I imagine Casa Azul was soothing to Kahlo, a painting she could look at and be salved faster than with any medicine.

When I first found Frida Kahlo's art, I was horrified. The

autobiographical viscera of a screaming woman cutting herself open from chest to abdomen or, even, when she was whole, the dedication to spending that much time looking into oneself, painting and repainting her image. I fell ill when I read, upon learning she would have no children, Kahlo used her pubic hair to paint with. I was young. I didn't understand a similar self-possession would overtake me.

For years, I was still trying to cosplay my way through the world as a healthy person, pretending I hadn't become crippled. In my changing state, "crippled" has become a word endeared to me: "severely damaged or malfunctioning," "someone who can't walk." For so long, I had no picture I could paint for someone else of my body. Because I didn't look like someone who lives with periods of paralysis—unpredictable times when I lose the use of my legs, my hands, or my whole left hemisphere—I felt obligated to play the role everyone else had assigned to me. Strong. But, in all aspects of life, I was learning I was more fragile in this world than I was allowed to let on. And so I found comfort in books like *The Secret Garden* in which children were overtaken by diseases like "consumption" and "rheumatism" that no one could account for, because the curious felt comfortable to me. I had my father show me pictures of hunchbacks, and other benign but troublesome tumors, from his copy of *Gray's Anatomy*, and asked a lot of questions about deformity. I was curious about what was going on inside me, and since I didn't know, I was trying to figure out how much time I had left. "It'll be fine," I have heard for years. For days, or weeks, or months, it will be. And then I collapse. My whole body unknown to itself—the muscles taut, the joints displaced—both, one, or the other.

I tried to be a perfect daughter. That morphed into being a capable, uncomplaining adult. But mostly what I did was overachieve so as not to be seen as overly sensitive, overly dramatic, weak for reasons out of my control. The truth was kept so deep inside, practically invisible.

I was lucky to have found surrealism; paintings with the bodies dripping with time. The distortion of the human form, bodies so wet with pain, time froze.

●

"Are you on time?" begins what is still one of my very favorite poems. Unpublished; the author unknown to me, the verses were just a piece of inspiration that my first love shared, back when we were teenagers, from a student in his undergraduate poetry workshop. I've forgotten the middle, but the poem ends: "marry everyone get married every day."

Pain has been my constant companion in life ("married every day"). There have been times when it felt absolutely impossible for anyone to love me, which is why I never blamed Frida for staying with a man who brought more pain to her than her illnesses ever had. What can I say? It was a different time. But also, when you are so small inside the hole of your body, it can feel good for someone so big and reticent to be opened. Someone reticent to be good.

Something people who don't live in excruciating pain don't know about the pain-body is that, sometimes, to be able to see the monster in your life on the outside, instead of always on the inside, is a huge relief. To be treated badly is to not be pitied—to be treated like you are any other person. It's probably something I shouldn't say, it's not a choice I've made for my own life, but I understand its source. In being disabled, diseased, you don't always want a moral high ground. You don't want to be seen as different just because your body requires more kindness. It's weird to say that abuse can make you feel ordinary. But ableism is so rampant and imperceptible in the ways it's ignored, it's nearly impossible for disabled people to participate in a world where they are not abused. We are abused by the medical system, which prioritizes pills over healing. We are abused by those close to us who ask more of us than we are capable of. We are abused of our value by a system that refuses to provide adequate accommodations for our talents. Economically, socially, medically—the monsters are all around us.

I see an honest, visceral survival in the cobalt scent of Frida Kahlo's clothes. I admire the freedom in her costuming because, aside from the love of blooming, there is a complete submission to the dresses and headdresses that make Mexican women exclusive models of the feminine exquisite. The way disabled Frida would position herself at the center of a womb, as an Eve, and as a form of perfection to guard the places of her worst injury. Securely guarded by feminine virtue. But in her peculiarity, this one side is never the whole. She stands in her own irony—the bisexual daughter of a deeply intellectual man whom she loved dearly; as much as she loved her own mustache, heavy eyebrow, and men's suiting. In her wholeness, she is more like me than I possibly realized I could be. We rarely get to celebrate disability as the mark of people who've cheated time of its chronology, that their existence is never binary—both infant and ancient in one setting. It's a reconciliation of human vulnerability. It means if one asks, "Are you on time?" that one has to account for the question of which timeline we're adhering to—the one we know eminently as our bodies, or the one that ticks. Time is slipping away from us much faster than we think.

•

Within the pages of Zadie Smith's *White Teeth* is a quote from one of her husband's poems. "Time is how you spend your love." I read this once while sick in bed and never forgot it. The place I felt most at home touring Casa Azul was Frida Kahlo's studio. Every inch of it a chronicle of the chronically ill, the pain of spinal surgery after surgery. The sequence didn't seem to have an aftermath—just a chronology. I recognized Frida Kahlo as someone I knew when I saw the full-size bed beside one empty easel twelve feet apart from a second full-size four-poster—the infamous one with a mirror attached, so she could still paint her self-portraits while recovering in bed. I understood the dizzying journey between art and rest, because for decades I've hidden from everyone the fact that in order for me to write, I have to sleep a significant amount of my life away.

In order to write I have to dream. In order to write I have to preserve my body. I am writing this at a moment when both of my legs have subluxated after a hard day of doing next to nothing. I did just a few steps of walking and an hour's worth of physical therapy. Dinner with a childhood friend I hadn't seen since I was a teenager. This was a good day. Some days are better or bigger, but time decides.

At dinner, my childhood friend said she imagined my days at a desk, my heart chattering away at a laptop into the wee hours of the evening. But today, it is only 10:18 a.m. and I'm in silk pajamas nestled in the covers of the king-size bed I keep soft with sheep's wool and linen. I dream. I wake up. I listen to my dreams. Before I rise I ask my body how much time it will need to make this day a long one. Sometimes there is no answer, so I lay a recorder to my chest and imagine your face and just tell you a story. I imagine your face, I just speak to you, like this, like now, and I feel more than surreal, opening the curtain to the underside of my reality.

I feel very frightened about how you might react.

All of a sudden, it seems deceptive that I've called this practice "writing" when today, in reality, my joints are too weak to do anything like that. When today, in reality, the only thing I can do now is lie in bed and free the lucid dream that I have something to say. But here we are. And we are so much closer together than we were when I was pretending to be an ordinary person. Because I have nothing left, I have nothing left to hide.

I can't tell you how much this hurts. Frida did. She opens up the shrieking viscera of her abdomen and inside I find her home, peaceful and stalwart, a world beyond breaking, a world beyond abuse. Sitting in her gardens, I say a silent prayer of thanks that today was a good day beside her grave. It's 2019. This will be the last trip I make out the country where I don't return in a wheelchair. But I keep traveling. Why?

I remember the part in *Frida*, the film where Salma Hayek, playing the artist, travels through her beloved city alive in a coffin. She's surrounded by flowers; a subtle joy creeps into her face. Whether or not we stop moving, we are always as close to death as we are to crawling our way out of it. That's what time is about. I don't worry about living in a way where I will be remembered. How do I want to live? In such a way that someone will be honored by how I die. The way I carried on. The way I carried the weight of my time here.

My body is cobalt blue when it stretches all over the world. Despite time not being on my side—*because* time is not on our side—I extend my fragile form around the Earth. I believe, as long as there is a world there must be someone to take in its erotic joys. On that journey, who could have told me there is nothing more erotic than my own mercy? To live, to let the clock run out on what I expect.

On Storytelling

Hoensbroek, Netherlands

Let me tell you a story:

In Dutch, there's only one letter's difference between "ghost" and "fairy tale." To me, that proximity between fright and pleasure feels very real. Maybe because I'm remembering back to when I was depressed. It was winter. We lived in a stone cottage on the edge of town, like in a storybook. Across the lane was a boerenwinkel, a farmers market, where the first ingredient in all the breads was butter and the eggs were always new. It sounds idyllic. In ways it was. But a gray permeated everything the sky touched and it was hard to shake off its film, like cold off snow. My sadness crawled under my skin and wriggled itself alive. I couldn't get warm. No matter the sun, a dark shadow inhabited all my thoughts. As I became more and more reclusive, I began to suspect that much of the unrest was also about my color.

I spent my first years in the Netherlands with the unrealistic expectation that I could be an ambassador for the world. I have bad boundaries. I take on too many responsibilities without asking for all the support I need. In return, staying positive had become exhausting. I approached much of the racism I encountered in the Netherlands with a mind-over-matter mentality. As if what happened to me could only affect me as much as I let it. But in the months that followed the tragic death of the refugee by fire, news from my home country reported the death of a young boy on a trip to the market. A gas station. A spookje and a sprookje—meaning a nightmare.

In the months that surrounded the death of Trayvon Martin, I barely had energy to move. I would wake up in the morning to defrost a chicken, turn on the broadband radio news, and wake up again, having closed my eyes for what was meant to be a minute and finding it had been hours—the light gone, the heavy crease of my sweatshirt printed in my cheek. Instead of trying to find comfort in the domesticity I once enjoyed, I decided to let the isolation permeate me.

Spookje or sprookje, I could be either one. When I was alone, I'd walk through the halls of my home listening to the bare touch of my fingers against the brightly painted walls, unaware of whether I was haunted by this foreign world or enchanted by it. It was jarring. I had never been so safe from the fear my life would end at the barrel of a gun. And I'd never felt more disturbed that it might not.

The one thing I was becoming more aware of in my late twenties was the abject loneliness of being a Black woman. Whether you are coupled or not, there is this strange displacement that comes from being Black and leaving childhood behind for good. Our time in the space of the innocent is always truncated. But the more I grew in my maturity the more I understood that my womanhood would always prove both outspoken and othered by the world in a way that made it impossible to truly feel a part of it. Strangely, even so, I felt called to protect it. There was a certain equality I started to demand for those I saw as unwanted, unrecognized by the world, with little regard for my own position—which was perilous. There was a recklessness in my discontent that, foreign country or not, I attribute to how being a Black woman is always a foreign feeling. Even when we're in the company of each other, there are so many moments when I find us brushing up to feel each other on all our haunches, uncertain if we will be taken into the fold.

Is the Black woman meant to be a solitary animal? In the Netherlands, I knew so few of us that lack of acceptance was less a concern than that our joint sorrows lacked an actual reprieve from seclusion. Especially in those months of death, I hoped that we'd strengthen each other in stories of frustration that unfurled into good things, like petals. Instead, each bad thing revealed another bad thing until every rose I'd hold crumbled under me.

I didn't want to talk about us dying. But in the center of town, I met with a dark-skinned Detroit woman visiting from Friesland—somewhere so white and so cold—and there was a strange enchantment in what we didn't say that permeated the ink of everything. The only time the people of the province remotely resembled her was during Christmas, when they covered their faces in soot, or black shoe polish, to parade around as Zwarte Piet, Santa's favorite slave. Going to the market with her young son, while her husband worked, a Dutchman in blackface stopped her dead, performing an apish jig before her coal-black body. She cried. In the eyes of the villain the fairy tale is always a nightmare.

Blackface is just one example. From what I've seen, it doesn't matter how many friends you have or how many places you've traveled or how much money you make. At least one time or another I've looked in the eyes of all Black women and seen the teary-eyed strain of someone trying to hold the world together, reconciling the ways it still fears her. The ways the world is terrifying and terrified by her. Wherever she is, and no matter her size or color in reality, she is always aware of the grace and bigness of her body, her brownness. The desire and fear attached to her touch. Her ferocious protection of anything close to her that might be weakness. The scar and woundedness of that work: you do not have to be a hurt Black girl to become a scarred Black woman, the mechanisms from which the world claws at you are many, varied, and acute.

Before we married, I made my husband promise I'd never live in our Netherlands home during December. But returning home in February only to find America a more frightening nightmare than the ghost of dead and dancing slaves was so hard for me I decided to hibernate until I could no longer feel the chill of winter. I was brown. And to keep me warm I grew a thin layer of fat and fur across my body.

When the doorbell rang, I would uncover myself from the bed upstairs but often be unfit for company. One time, a constellation of pimples took over the side of my face and I'd covered them in toothpaste the night before, mostly to punish my husband with my lack of interest in being presentable in a world so ugly. I tried to go to the doctor but she claimed I was suffering from isolation, not depression, and so there was no pharmacy solution for what was wrong with me. After my brief talk with the woman from Detroit, I blamed my husband for what I hadn't known about how deeply I'd feel my race in the Netherlands, because I wanted to feel as if he'd tricked me. It was hard to accept this was a fate I'd chosen for myself, because it had been so hard to watch the uptick in crimes against Black people, by the police and otherwise, since President Obama had been elected. I don't know why I saw a European country as a way out of this. Fewer guns? Fewer people?

But I became silent and dramatic about what I couldn't change in my environment. I wanted him, and everyone close, to witness the harshness of what the world had made of me—a slovenly beast. I never asked if he should love me inside of that urge. I didn't know how.

Two of our neighbors, both Englishwomen, would check in on me regularly knowing the sadness solemnity can breed in a dark Dutch winter. I yawned, and invited them in and fired up the kettle before finally touching the white sticky frost still on my face. I was frightened by how polite they were in the face of how unkempt I was. I excused myself to wash my face. I looked in the glass. It troubled me that so much of what is a true fairy tale depends entirely on your perception of it. Was I the witch or the maiden? I asked myself, squinting into the mirror. I returned to the kitchen, where my guests were seated, a cleaner domesticated animal.

It became pretty normal, when I was at home pouring cups of tea, that the conversation would steer somewhere toward bears. In Limburg, people were obsessed with bear stories. It was strange to me. Bears were things I never thought about, but in the southern Dutch perception of my neighbors they overran the streets of America, tearing down civilization in every place they touched. Brown, black, or otherwise, I knew nothing about them, but my neighbors were insatiable for a knowledge I didn't have.

"How are they with pets?"

"What's it feel like when they roar?"

"When they're after you, you run straight or zigzag?"

For a while it felt as if every time I turned there was someone in Limburg, looking up toward me with blinking eyes, expecting me to answer questions I couldn't. At first I was clear there was nothing I knew about bear handling, having spent most of my life in cities. But the more they pressed, and the sadder I became, sharing bear stories became the delirious cure to my loneliness.

My two English neighbors stirred milk into their mugs and over the tinny stir of their teaspoons started talking about an episode of a National Geographic television show where the host, a two-hundred-pound man in a four-hundred-pound cage, tempted a ferocious grizzly with a piece of fried chicken. "Man, I gotta admit, I'm a little intimidated," he said as the bear knocked the cage to its side. I cackled like a witch while they retold the tale because it reminded me of every stereotypical first date with a Black woman in America. Fried chicken. Intimidation. Finished with a slap.

"Truthfully, he should have fed her rare meat," I said to my neighbors, lifting the new teakettle as it screeched. "Bears prefer game to cooked picnic baskets."

And my neighbors said, "Ahhh . . . ," as if what I'd offered was full of wisdom. No matter how stupid or mundane the fact I shared, the response would always be like that.

It was weird. I know. But it gave me a reason to keep going.

It gave me something to be other than the surly, Black American housewife. So I would load up the podcast app with every bear story I could find on NPR and survey them during my cross-country runs for facts to drop into the conversation, even when I wasn't asked to be an expert.

Dark, hairy, unpredictable. The North American terrorist. Dangerous on all fours but savage on two legs. There was an obvious kinship I felt with the bear and the story of the bear as a Black person in a foreign country. For some time after I moved, I felt like a fixation for the people who didn't understand me. I was like them, in that I was human—drank the same drinks and carried the same casserole dishes to neighborhood occasions—but I was unlike them. In ways no one could put their finger on. It wasn't just about my being from a different country. The way I moved, the way they felt on guard every time I shifted, as if preparing for an attack—this was familiar to me but new in their minds.

Part of the reason I'd wanted to leave the US during Obama's early years, other than the increase in Black fatalities, was because of the cloying way liberals enjoyed congratulating themselves for voting in the most popular presidential candidate during an economic recession. Up in Harlem, where I lived, Black people were being evicted from their homes left and right. Downtown, where I worked, men with homes in New Jersey stood around the office patting themselves on the back for electing a Black president while putting us office workers on three-quarters pay, and then half time. They said it couldn't be helped. But one of my Haitian coworkers intercepted a fax about sets of French doors being added to my boss' home renovation that cost more than my coworker's salary.

I loved that the Obamas existed, but I lost my allegiance early when it came to the potential that my place in my country would change. I built naïve fantasies around being whisked away to the lands where most fairy tales happened as if I could partake in them. Along with socialized healthcare and a sustainable living wage—treasured fantasies when America was going through the Great Recession. I'd say I'd forgotten myself, but I didn't know myself yet. I didn't know that being married would take away from me the protection girlhood provided, to be outspoken, or cute and "precocious," because as a married woman I no longer represented youth. I was now the halfway mark between the princess and the crone. Silly me. No fairy tales are written about what happens after everyone moves inside the castle, especially when you awake one morning as the big brown hulking thing under the covers in a town full of Goldilocks.

It is obvious that I wondered if Limburg insisted on discussing bears with me because, when they saw me, it was the only thing they could think about. They wanted to know if I found pets tasty. If, when I was angry, I roared. And what was the best way to run away from me, if it came down to it. Since

I had no satisfactory answers to these questions myself yet, I made things up.

"Once in high school when we were camping," I told my in-laws (in high school, I never went camping), "a grizzly bear came up to us" (there are no grizzly bears in Kentucky), "and we just started talking to her, really low and slow, you know, like 'Hey, bear, you don't wanna eat us, my barn jacket's not gonna taste very good'" (because, from what I knew from the news, most of the time all you had to do to avoid bear attacks was keep your distance and leave them alone). My in-laws passed a serving dish of hot boiled potatoes, hanging on my every word. They were great fans of folk wisdom.

"And then what happened?" my mother-in-law asked, hoping for some grand ferocity. Looking back, I can only imagine how the scene might have seemed to them, the possibility us two brown, terrifying entities might roar the pants off one another. In reality, the story I'd stolen that night was intentionally anticlimactic. To get the bears to disappear this is all the campers had had to do. I'd grown wary of being scary, and wanted to show that maybe, with a little understanding, bears weren't really bears in the way that we feared them to be. And maybe, in some tiny way, I hoped that I wasn't. I wanted to come closer to my family than the stories that weren't my own that I'd use to feed their curiosity. But there was no hunger for that type of lore. I learned the story of a beast entering one's midst is always supposed to reward suspicions. Who is a hero without a story of survival?

But then I'd think of the teenage boy, his hand, brown, and sticky with candy. I'd remember him and get sick, holding a napkin to my mouth.

"Are you okay?" my mother in-law would say, pulling the dinner pot from its trivet, telling me to press a boiled potato from the supper dish onto my throat, my gut, whatever it was that ailed me. It wasn't unusual for my mother-in-law to believe that almost anything could be cured by compressing a warm potato on it. But not my thoughts. Who were we now that a normal man could kill a teenage boy in Florida and we eat dinner like nothing had changed? Was he a ghost? Was this a nightmare? Am I?

In that moment, it was easier in my pain to be the witch, conjuring a story that was mischievous, stupid, and playful. I gave them the ending they desired, something loud and unpleasant, and they settled into their stroopwafels, satisfied. When we left, I felt strong, like I had batted a fish from a river with my own big paw. But the fantasy was quick and futile.

"Why do you keep lying?" my husband asked in a tone that was mostly concerned.

I smiled when I answered him: "Because it brings me pleasure."

Stoking their prejudices at a time when I felt scared made me feel powerful. There was something manic and sad in that desire. If I couldn't change the ways I was a terrible animal, I could at least control what attention was paid toward me. In my smile, I bare my teeth. I wish I'd understood how unhealthy I'd become then. But sometimes, when you care, it feels as if this world only offers people of color the choice of madness. Unlike on the world band radio that I stayed glued to, the mention of Trayvon Martin on the Dutch news was nothing beyond a headline, a moment in the ever-changing landscape of Western politics. I had stopped to listen. But the world wouldn't change because of one teenager.

I was lying because it was impossible to bring up the subject of Trayvon Martin without my Limburg neighbors trivializing it into "a Black thing," one of the grossest and most irritating of European dismissals. And even those who tried to empathize lacked the context to understand why trying to explain the hurt I felt made me so frustrated.

"Did you know him?" asked my English neighbor, outstretching her hand, trying to understand why the death of one person, heard over the radio, would send me into a months-long depression. I wanted to say, "I am hibernating because I have grown tired of how dangerous some of us are considered simply for existing."

But I didn't have the energy to be that honest. I said, "Yes." Was that a lie? Although I never knew him, did I not now know his ghost in the truncation of what his story should be? It was easier to insulate myself in bears than to talk about how I was actually feeling. How much their ignorance felt cruel, and angered me. And the more I spoke of bears, the more I felt like one, the more my timid sadness felt entitled to snarl and mark its territory.

Sometimes I'm a beast. It's unfortunate. I try not to be. And sometimes, I don't. At times, I think it is important for people to understand I am someone to be scared of. As a Black woman, it's hard not to bear the tragedies of our people even when you have borne no children. But the fear we conjure when we bear our truths is dangerous. We are so much more likely in speaking up to be typecast as arrogant, difficult, angry, or crazy. In our fairy tales, the mirror is always distorted. Are we the innocent or the villain? The answer is always skewed; the world is unable to look at us honestly. The world is often incapable of deciphering our roar as something necessary to hear. What if the bear is never lying? What if all our cries have truth in them?

In a bear video that went viral a white woman attacked a set of brown bears invading her bricked-in backyard as they threatened her dogs. It's hard not to cheer for her victory. The incident felt so pure and understandable—sometimes, when we are scared to lose something, it's impossible to frame logic around what we'd do to protect it. According to the CDC, the top three threats to human life are unintentional injury, homicide, and suicide, making the biggest threat to people, people. And yet, it's bear attacks that fascinate us. The implausible, the unlikelihood that something foreign is waiting to drag us into its dark. Compared to the hundreds of thousands of instances of death-by-people, bear attacks are a minuscule sum—around one hundred or less in the US, twice as many in Europe. But the most significant detail about bear attacks I've found is that 50 percent are attacks mother bears make in defense of their cubs. Meaning, the desire to protect is a common metaphor. Our most overlooked attributes are the ones we hold in common. We let our fear stand in place of understanding. But why, when we are so similar in the difficult things we do in the name of love? When we first encounter a stranger, I want the simultaneity between "us" and "them" to be clearly seen. That, for the most part, we all want the same thing—to not be meat. To share something more than inoculative pleasantries with the people we call neighbors. The black woman in me says that we are all family. I want language that upholds our divineness and destroys our divisiveness. We are family. It is our duty to call our people in, call them out, and call them to arms.

Much like the myth in the danger of bears, many Black women, femmes, and nonbinary people are singled out in their jobs, homes, and neighborhoods for being a disruption. In fighting for the same metaphysical truths of all humans. But given the way we've been written into the script, it's hard to believe that an embodied life is not a delusion. I mean, I understand bears. All the certainty I hold as a beautiful, solitary animal slips away when I see them take in the petrifying foreignness of my flesh. I bat my paw in the river, what little I can do to change its tide feels futile—in the world, in one rural Dutch province. The best I can do is feed myself. Every time I sit down to write a story, I think about the fears that tear us apart and keep us unnourished, that we are afraid of what will happen one day if a Black woman raises a voice that roars. If that roar brings down an avalanche across civilization. As if raw chaos is not the sound in nature that organizes and softens into peace.

It is winter and we are the noise. I am tired, I'm hungry, and in the midst of my roar. I want to eat the dead thing alive in me that doesn't want to be a Black bore anymore. No longer the bright fear in a black hole. No longer a growl rendered a sharp weapon. I want to kill the bleak thing in me that can't help but react to a rattled cage. I want to be just one large, soft, resting animal. But we're not there yet. The story is still being written with my paw to the barrel of a pistol and a rifle pointed at my head. We need me to be odd and dangerous. And I am. In the cold I roam the earth as a predator until we are no longer prey. I hope I don't die this way.

In the Netherlands, at my pristine kitchen table, I take out a dictionary and look up the word "bear" for the first time, a word I never assumed I needed to know because I knew it well. I was surprised to find "bear" is a euphemism, the world's oldest. That the word we use just means "brown one." Early German tribes were so terrified of the large brown creatures they encountered in the woods that they made speaking the word for them taboo so as to not conjure their appearance. And so who "bears" were has been lost forever to our collective memory. That's the lesson. It's that deceptively simple. I have to roar, no matter how dangerous it makes me feel. Because all it took was one story—one story—for an entire brown being to be erased.

How dangerous does a bear have to be to have its name lost to everyone? Not much. All it had to do was come out of the forest. Shake itself off. And stand up.

On Beauty

For DMC. A beginning.

Venice, Italy

Witnessing the beautiful is always the petite death. We say we are awed, stupefied, entranced. For a moment, we forget there's anything else worth paying attention to. We are what we feel and we feel enchanted. "Enchanted" is a word that once meant "emit sound." "Encantare." To sing. That's exactly what beauty does. It's not just that we see beauty: it rings, in our ears, like iron in a bell tower, it wakes us and ends us. The cycle of life and death is present in everything beautiful we see.

Beauty is frightening and delightful, as the way the water-bus crashes into the dock in Venice. Its song is beauty; you're holding on to whatever you can, for dear life, but the weight of the boat still overtakes you. Shakes you, as the attendant in his black gloves ties the boat to the dock with a heavy rope. All the people jostle to exit, you are happy you have survived, you leave, and you turn around to look back as the beauty you just traveled—the water—consumes you. Old-milk pink and pastel. It'd be dangerous—deadly for you to enter it. Having fallen in during the shoot for the film *Summertime* in 1955, Katharine Hepburn never recovered. The infection she got from falling in (love) lasted the rest of her life—she lived to be ninety-six—(love) is how Peggy Guggenheim committed suicide.

So rumored. When Peggy leapt off her personal canal to swim the Adriatic, she was in her eighties, death coming for her one way or the other. She chose "by baptism"; the official record says "a stroke." Meaning, it doesn't matter if you sink or swim. In the minds of those who know Venice, falling in love is falling in.

In spite, or because, of its infectiousness, the water looks watercolor perfect. Rightly so, it's filled with centuries of refuse, abandoned art. The way the city was built was also beauty filled: legend is, instead of continuing to fight for the edge of a coastline as marauders kept coming ever closer, the early Venetians just . . . built a new one. They imagined a new place to live and fashioned a way to design it. To build land. That we still marvel at this, have no clear sense how this was done, is enchantment. It moves me to song.

I hope we never know. I hope Venice disappears, reclaimed by the opaque waters, before we ever find out. In death beauty serves its purpose. We must remember that beauty is never a guarantee. I love when old Italian women talk about "la grande bellezza" they were in their day, perhaps carrying in their billfolds a copy of celluloid that proves it. The great beauty. Beauty can be copied but not preserved; we should never stay beautiful forever. It is disturbing to think of it. There is no humility in it. Although I want to believe otherwise, I have learned humanity is meant to scar us, something ugly must befall us in order for us to say we've truly lived.

•

When I first arrived in Venice, I thought "cosmopolitan" was a hooded trench coat from Old Navy and a pair of maroon cowboy boots. I was twenty-one; I'd never lived anywhere that fit into an ocean. I fancied myself that kind of person for whom space could run small but its tributaries deep. There was nothing I didn't feel connected to in Venice, so tiny and yet much of the world congregated there. In art, there was magic in every corner; the city sang to me.

The first night I arrived, I ran the streets after midnight, as I would repeatedly, taking flight over the bridges in my "cosmopolitan" clothes. Why would I run in the middle of the night in a coat and cowboy boots? Because I wanted to. Because the city was open to it. Because the city was open to me. At that hour, I was alone with the scuffle of my boots hitting the hard cobblestone, making music, my heart heavy. I was alive.

I was alive as I had been nowhere else. I could feel it. I went to Venice to study architecture; I learned from my very first water-bus ride that the best way to engage the city's architecture was at night. At night, when it was lit up inspirational, like every palazzo was Cinderella's palace at Disney World. From the bus, I traced all the shadowed intricacies of their faces, their mouths perilously gulping water as the bus stirred the break. On the water-bus, every time we descended under a bridge, I'd say a quick prayer. On my night runs, I would say a quick prayer before sprinting across them. I kept my feet light and my wishes fleet. I was worried the bridge would crumble over us or I would stumble onto it—my teeth breaking like piano keys. The dangerous beauty in falling (in love).

I had never grown up feeling like a beautiful person. Growing up where I did, I felt I stuck out in ways that were dangerous. I didn't always believe I'd survive all the ways the world worked to make me feel small and disposable—how long can you go holding an emerald inside of you and hide it? I think that's why I ran, so I could keep the ways I glittered and re-fracted. That's why I loved Venice. It's a jewelry box meant to withstand its own gorgeousness. Humanity does not like to be upstaged but, in Venice, believing yourself beautiful in its image is humility. Seeing yourself as beautiful is not competing.

At the end of my run, I was hungry. I'd never eaten in Italy and all my tastes were commercial. I sat down, just after midnight, at a red checkered laminate table. A tourist trap. I chose spaghetti Bolognese off of the picture menu because it reminded me of my childhood watching *Lady and the Tramp*. The waiter served me in a white shirt and bow tie, a towel on his forearm to complete the ambience, but the meal came out microwaved and I ate my flat, dry pasta unaware that there would be meals in Venice I would never recover from—their little death delighting my insides—but this one I wouldn't forget. I thanked the waiter, finished my tiny glass of wine, and laid down a few euro coins as tip.

I went back into the city, headphones on my ears, hands in my pockets, ready to run until my coat flew like the cape of a superhero. I slowed down on the last bridge home. Leaning over the bridge staring out into the water alone was a Lady— a tiny stuffed Disney cocker spaniel. I took it as a good omen. I took her home. I sat her in the windowsill where she could always look out at the canal and have it sing to her.

Sooner or later I started dating the beautiful man who owned a gondola. He developed the habit of singing up to me from the canal, to the window where Lady waited. That was a beautiful story. I'm embarrassed to say I fell, in love, in the most obvious way. In Venice, romance carries such simplicity— such humility—I forget how rare it is everywhere else. Is it conceited for me to say I've had more romance than I dreamed of? I hope that's something I can share and cherish. I met the man who owned the gondola on the bridge that marked my way to college. He would marvel at me. "Che bellissima," or "Che bella donna."

Having the language of beauty applied to me would leave me so terribly scared. I'd learned how to trick myself. Despite the emerald I'd been holding I still believed I wasn't worth noticing. Youth is silly. I had been in love before, but the difference in meeting the gondolier was that the beauty belonged to me—a possessive, not an adjective. "Bella" an article, of clothing, I never took off; my tone, my texture, the length of my fingers all equally beautiful on their own—not because someone loved me but because I was. But also because I loved. He was a beautiful man. Still is, a bit ageless. I walked past him once at midnight on a visit to Venice, in my early thirties. He was escorting two young women and I pretended to be taken in by the glass glittering in a store window. I stared into his reflection in a goblet, a small gold Adonis from the sea.

Back in my twenties, the American students in my study abroad program would jealously call the gondolier Jordache because his face contained all the pretty angular cuts from an eighties jean advertisement. And somehow, I was ashamed of this. It wasn't just my own beauty I was immune to. I laughed with them—chicken skinned and ordinary; it felt important for me to hide my conceit. Was it conceited to love the beautiful man who came and sang under my window calling me "donna"? Lady. Me and the stuffed brown doll listening to his song from the window of a palace apartment. How could I not? Life is a fairy tale. It's just no one's skin is brown when they're written down. I take this moment literally, I imbibe it,

I write it down; I share its enchantment as often as necessary. I think it's important for us all to remember:

We don't become beautiful until we believe it.

Venice took me out onto a boat and showed me all the world's beauties. Secretly locked in, the city treated me as if I was as precious as jewels, as gold, even if I could never afford them. Knowing what you are worth makes you look at the world differently.

●

I kept coming back. Every time I stepped back in the city it would find me a new story, cut and composed for the person I was now. My second visit was when I interned at the Peggy Guggenheim Collection. A museum in the smallest palazzo of all of Venice—smallest as in short, because its base was so grand it would have obviously overtaken the two palaces on either side of it. (Not all competition is accepted.) The neighboring palaces set city ordinances to make sure the building would never be completed. Nobody wanted the stubby kingdom except an American: beauty.

When I moved back to Venice, I didn't tell Marcello I was coming. We weren't together during a time when orbiting each other on social media as lovers that once happened was much of a practice. I missed him, but after a while I grew comfortable in leaving the subtle romance of whether we'd ever again encounter each other up to fate. At the museum, at sundown, the first event I worked at night entertaining dozens of artistic dignitaries, he was there. Among all the long boats, oiled and decorated, and while my beloved loaded his passengers into his gondola, I watched. A coincidence—there was no reason for him to look around and imagine I'd be there, and yet, there I was—he didn't notice me. Venice is always a fairy tale, even if it doesn't feel like it's the right one. He took a lady by the hand and she descended into the gilded black boat, her ring finger adorned in emeralds, and that was that. They floated away. My world was his no more. Although I tried several times to reconnect the pages, the story was completed. Beauty is fleeting but its absence can make you an entirely different person. There is beauty in this and newness. In letting the gone gleam through.

My second life was my first's death. I met a music prodigy, Syrian. We were both African; he told me so. We met at the Biennale's opening party for the African pavilion, a DJ Spooky concert. He said I danced like the women he knew from home—a song—I was home to someone. Finally home in a foreign country. He always wore a suit and hat—like Fellini. I felt like celluloid every time he kissed me. We'd ride on the waterbus under the moon, the motor tick-ticking like eight millimeter. A film that just kept rolling. We were the two most beautiful brown things in the world, and we had found each other. A tiny, beautiful courtship—of course I died when he left me.

I forgave him for years and years; it wasn't meant to last. Last time I was in Venice, still trying to figure out how to turn this fairy tale into something larger, he met me in the bar of the cosmopolitan hotel I stayed at overlooking the Adriatic. He'd graduated from suits to linen trousers and white button-downs, it was summer, we walked the city like we were fifteen years younger and I was still healthy. He held up my arm like a beau instead of like a crutch, and we shared old narratives. Adding to them sweet footnotes we'd forgotten the first time. He took me under the window of a grand hotel where he had played the grand piano in order to put himself through college.

He told me the story of how, when he was thirteen, he ran barefoot through the streets of Damascus—from the refugee camp his family lived in to the post office—to submit his application for the Italian international school that brought him here. Nobody told him to. How did he come to believe in that beautiful fire that told him *the world is yours?* I marvel at him.

He played the grand piano in the grand hotel window because he was meant to study music. But he worried there would be no emerald in it, and so work became the only place to hear his song. He studied engineering. He never became an engineer. But under the window the city would congregate at the end of his hotel shifts. At the bench. Sometimes listening, sometimes waltzing, always clapping.

His story is sweet in my fingers, like ice cream. Like Venice is all ice cream. Like all there is, is ice cream—like there is nothing else to eat. So sweet, the chill so painfully cold it kills the roof of you. You delight in waiting for it to warm. Back at the Peggy collection, a museum friend of mine—Iggy—and I made a pact to go to each gelateria and eat one scoop of ice cream. It was research. We were excavating the city to find which had the most beautiful ice cream. Iggy was beautiful, "macondo," he would say as a babe, making up a Tagalog word—he was Filipino, raised in Rome, son of an ambassador. He knew his way around Italian, French, English, and sweet milk. He had a formula: the best way to tell who had the best gelato was to pick the simplest flavor for comparison. Vanilla. Sometimes pear. Pear was my favorite, translucent, the lightest emerald, and hard to come by. It was like biting into an icy piece of fruit—"The joy in it!" I said to him, humming; delicious beauty moves me to music.

On our ice cream runs it was Iggy who pointed out how often the men of the city would call out how beautiful I was. "Che bellissima creatura!" one cried out just as I was denying it, as if to prove Iggy's point. He turned to me, amused and infuriated that I couldn't hear how often the city sang of me. Not just sang to me. God—why did I ever leave—I was so loved?

Beauty and love have almost absolutely nothing to do with each other. Being a beautiful creature has never stopped anyone from leaving me.

But I always come back to Venice. Never in sequence, always recursive, always some brand-new beautiful beginning.

There is no last time, but the last time I'm remembering I brought my best friend. He bought a small guitar he called "baby" from a glass storefront window and we played music for food. We befriended the old owner of a restaurant called Paradise Lost—the sound system was shit but the fritto misto crackled warm between our teeth. We were pleased the store owner complained that he'd "never seen a worse performance." I smiled. It was beautiful to be bad at something. To oversell. And still he took us out on his bright red boat, the motor's music hot and sweet. On the water, beauty becomes virtuosic. Violins. I want to repeat and repeat and repeat the intervals like cantos. I fell in love with a me who loved me back. I fell in love with whoever helped me love me.

This time, it was the man who stood beside me playing guitar—my brother, my best friend—we took him for ice cream. Amarena. Sour cherry. And when the cold gelato hit the house of his mouth for the first time he hummed and I could hear the enchantment taking over him the same way it had sung into me—a groundswell. We don't speak anymore. Him, me, or the city. No—the city still comes back to me in a series of returns, an oar pushing my long black boat through the ocean. Venice keeps me moving, its beauty so irreconcilable I understand why beautiful things can last forever and I thank him. I thank them all, imagining a sinking, floating world that still consumes me. If beauty lasted forever, we wouldn't need it. If beauty lasted at all, we'd all forget.

On Sex

At some point, we are going to recognize that we are all the people. That we are all that's left. In a world where we are both so tethered to and so unbound from tradition, there is no greater pleasure than other people, no greater pleasure for ourselves. We forget that we are people. We forget there is no greater honor somebody can give than their body's willing pleasure paired with ours. It doesn't have to be sexual, but it is. There is no specific organ that is sexual. Isabel Allende said, "The best aphrodisiacs are words, the g-spot is in the ears," and for years, I was giddy for sweet talking. Shouldn't that affection we feel be the affection we are willing to give ourselves? Shouldn't that sweet talk be mutual? Shouldn't we feel in our skins the same way we feel wrapped up around each other? Alone or together, we are folded and infinite. We remember the twinkling lights of ourselves moving through time.

I believe we have come far enough in civilization that sex is no longer a tool of procreation. Sex is an act of warfare. Sex is a political act. Just think of it. In all the dangers we've encountered by now through the simple act of touching—we touch now for all of the life we can't take back. Think of all that we didn't deserve because we wasted it. If we don't touch each other now, what did we save ourselves for?

If we didn't love to touch ourselves. If we didn't learn that loving to touch ourselves was a secret. Was it our own pleasure that shielded us from the war we witnessed—the war we survived? We are all soldiers in the army of each other's freedom. Each time we wash hands to hold hands. Each time we washed our hands. Each time we clapped for the people who might not come home to the people they loved to make love to. We love ourselves and so we love each other, I know it. Because I do.

I did.

•

Today's story is brought to you by the American healthcare system. A tragedy, a love affair—mostly with myself. I was standing in a bikini the day a retired medical chief told me I was dying. Shivering, my nipples hardening, waist-deep in a swimming pool with the phone to my ear. He said it the way you'd tell someone their brake pads need replacing. Like I was replaceable.

"Well, it sounds like you're dying," he said, "or at least, people in your stage of a diagnosis don't usually live past forty-five." I had just turned thirty-nine. I didn't know this kind of prognosis delivery could be typical of doctors with critical patients they don't understand—it's either "nothing" is wrong or "nothing" can be done. Death being their strongest prescription for a solution. This was the first day I learned this—a tragedy. This was my first day crossing over to the other side of the medicinal justice system, from presumed healthy to proven guilty.

It would also take me a while to learn that "guilty" is a verdict so many people are suffering under in silence. All in a system where an unfit body is the alienating prison for anyone deemed chronically, disablingly unwell.

Each sentencing is specific. Hypermobile Ehlers-Danlos syndrome was mine. A genetic disorder had been attacking my joint tissue like the fall of Rome, like what John Green said of falling in love, like what Ernest Hemingway said about going bankrupt: "gradually, then suddenly," "slowly, then all at once." The specialists I visited referred to this as an "impressive presentation." Not a death sentence, in the long run, but a death threat. Life in prison where there was once free life.

"There is nothing we can do to keep your joints from detaching from your muscles," said the second doctor I called, a pediatric Ehlers-Danlos expert. But by then both my knees were dislocating when I stood up and my fingers were popping in and out of their sockets when I turned on the faucet and washed the dishes. My left eye was dislodging by the time I found a doctor who said the one thing that kept me together: "Your condition is treatable, just complex."

None of this is sexy. Although, I do look good in an eye patch. "Like the bitch Cruella de Vil is afraid of," a friend WhatsApped me after I sent him a photo of my covered eye paired with my obligatory beachfront-living attire, another bikini. I modeled for myself in a full-length mirror. I looked hot as a Marvel villain: Thanatos.

This was the beginning of my diving into the erotic dichotomy of the American medical narrative: we crave deformity but loathe the people who survive it in real life. Look at our superheroes; disability is our kink. Each mutant and spy we glorify shows the acuity of autism, the inhibitions of madness, or the heightened sensory capacities of an injury—whether they were born that way or changed en route. Our stories make these people magical, supernatural. We mask our fears of affliction with stories of invulnerability, but the glory doesn't hold when the mask comes off.

But you're not here for the sadness, you're here for the sex. So let's go back to the fact that I never looked hotter than when my eye was falling out. There was an erotic dichotomy to my

Ehlers-Danlos. Like an origin story, EDS took control of my hormones and started pumping my body up in a superhuman ecstasy. A wonder. My blood was filled with pregnancy hormones; I was not pregnant.

"Your joints are going lax because your body believes you are about to give birth," said my physical therapist.

"Don't be alarmed if you start lactating, but if you do, call me!" said the doctor who'd save my life.

"Like a fertility goddess," the skinny, pensive lover said. A hyperloop engineer I met in the hot tub of my Marina del Rey apartment complex, the Pearl, a spacious, run-down three-story that had been a swingers' spot during the eighties—where Oprah had rented out the third floor to have parties and Anne Bogart had once been put up by the Getty—a five-minute walk from Venice Beach. The swingers reputation was long gone, but the apartments, like most of the coast in Los Angeles, was populated by *Baywatch*-looking singles. The engineer wasn't one of them. He was lanky, with a stippled beard, and smoked black-label Marlboro cigarettes. It was a brief, sweet affair. I was lying on the bed, still in my swimsuit, taking calls in real time from medical experts while he ran his long fingers along the traces of hot tub bubbles still on my leg.

There was no separation for me between sex and sickness.

What I normally would have hidden from a lover to preserve some sense of beauty, I could not. The day I met him, I'd been wearing the eye patch and a gold bikini like *Black Mirror* Wonder Woman. The disease was not static but circular. By the time we went on our first date I was in leg braces and knee-high cheerleading socks. Fetish items. It was close enough to Halloween, I could have been trying out different costumes. I assured him I was not.

But I was.

It was a time of little pleasure. A sexual fascination with the strange weakness of my body was somewhat desirable to me. I began to look at the number of prosthetics I'd increasingly need with the same raw awe as I did the riding crops and laces I associated with burlesque. I'd always loved how those performers teetered on the edge of frailty and power.

"Having EDS is like being a ballerina," explained my physical therapist. "You balance all your weight on your weakest points as if you're always en pointe."

The metaphor was helpful. I didn't have to be "sick." I could be Dita Von Teese. A rare feminine engine. I marveled at my prosthetics: their tightness, sheen, and webbing. The pelvic brace that cinched my waist, the leg braces that steeled my gait, the eye patch that focused my gaze. The arm sling and fingerless gloves—all black—looked almost elegant when viewed from the right direction. And the pièce de résistance, a neck brace—of which I had two—had a cyborg Frida Kahlo quality in its own right.

"I feel like a Dalí painting," I'd said to my physical therapist.

We were learning my symptoms were more complicated than typical EDS. My body was like wax melting and hardening. Limp, then paralytic. Like surrealist art.

"Yes," he said, "that's a clear way to put it." But there were more medical terms. The constellation of my EDS included a movement disorder, dystonia, like Parkinson's and multiple sclerosis. A constellation. That's what medical professionals often call a group of symptoms that have no clear pattern of connection but present at the same time. I imagined stars charting a path through my joint tissue. Burning bright, then cold—temporarily but achingly, painfully so.

But there was still something distinctly sexual about all my limits and contorting. It reminded me of making things. Of creation. Art is joy in joy, and joy in tragedy. So I played with my illness, mixing the palette of both like paint. I took portraits pairing my sexy, sick body with prosthetics and lingerie. My boundaries of beauty dissolved. I felt like Kali, the goddess of fertility—and destruction. Why wouldn't I? Her name means "She Who Is Black." I felt both deathly and puerile. I was fragile, like a baby in its prettiness, its beauty and adaptation to weakness. On those days when the disease was cyclical—not static—I'd need all of my arsenal to keep myself together, my limbs almost multiple. I must have looked a fright. The fact I was no longer my same self was slightly intoxicating. For a moment the presence of death felt like a large beating heart in my hands. The transition felt holy. In my reverence, I repeated the only lines I knew from the Bhagavad Gita: "Now I am become death, the destroyer of worlds."

And I needed sex. Like all gods. Or learned, after I woke up from my first morning after my first, that I could walk again. A miracle as I lay lugubriously in bed, basking in the beauty of my naked legs, sending "JESUS WALKS!!" GIFs to my closest friends. I think about this a lot with dick-having people. The complete, proud bewilderment of what a vaginal organ is capable of. I consider this real faith. I went in for a checkup.

"Is there anything that alleviates your symptoms?" my doctor asked as she hit my knees with a tiny rubber hammer. I grumbled one word out the side of my mouth.

"I'm glad you told me sex helps your symptoms," said my doctor days later (like a scientist, clinically, whimsically). "It means your profile of the disease is dopamine responsive." Dopamine and oxytocin, a nutritionist would confirm. Meaning the cure for what was killing me was the love hormones, the cuddle hormones, the feel-good hormones. My doctor finally laughed, "I can't give you a prescription for that."

While the hyperloop lover showers in his bathroom, I think about our chemical bonds. On his work desk, an assortment of pharmacy vials. He frets a lot about his trouble concentrating, his bouts of depression, and his heart-racing sleeplessness. I don't check, but assume each prescription matches his story as much as mine does. I've still got several rounds of blood tests. I've been prescribed nothing yet.

My unmedicated body is warm chaos. I flirt around him in bed in a sheer black feathered teddy and neck brace. A calm, passionate coming apart. He kisses my neck and I tell him I think about getting tattoos of covalent bonds behind my ear. "Where?"

I trace invisible molecules. He climbs over me and kisses those too. I won't say that it's love, it's science. I tell him, there's a deep kinship in death drive and sex drive—like the myth of Persephone—one foot in the underworld, a seed in one's mouth.

Today, sex is brought to you in pill form—each hell-seed in the pomegranate. Persephone and Hades, the forbidden fruit whose seed leads straight to the underground. A Greek tragedy. And yet, we eat. We try to escape but our fate is sealed. It's how we treat medicine. It's how we treat sex. We don't want to be wanting. We want to feel good as soon as possible. We say, "You need to get laid," like it's some sort of prescription. We know sex as the cure for what kills us. But that's not why we say it. We say it because we don't want to hear what hurts.

But both death and sex make us wax poetic, as if we aren't turned on until we reach an edge. In the ecstasy of my pain, my senses intensify. My synesthesia climaxing so the world is constantly breaking into prisms.

This was the thing I loved about him, the hyperloop lover.

He was the first person I'd had who had the same symptom, empathy. It's hard to describe the synesthesia surrounding purple, but we'd cuddle and stare at the lightbulb while he described what swapping out one feeling for another feeling felt like in his body—math equations coming together before him like Picassos, which is how I feel language—and I told the story my way, whatever's inside makes music pour out like light.

Like orgasms. Erotic pleasure has always let me see colors, each type of orgasm distinct in its spectrum and taste. I'd only shared this about me once, with my last boyfriend—six months before. We'd try something new and I'd tell him the color. Our standard configuration, dark red. I was constantly injured. I didn't know I was sick but I got much better. When he left me, he told me: "How could I make a life with anyone whose body is doing what yours does?"

This is the erotic irony. After decades of romance and traveling, I'd grown accustomed to the idea I'd never settle down or be taken care of. Not because I didn't want to, but because of the life I was born into. There's a strong singularity expected of Black women in this culture—a stoicism, an alienation of affection, an ongoing expectation of infinite self-reliance. But then I found myself with a disease with a cure almost too simple for me to hope for. It was a hard pill to swallow. If somebody loved me, I would get better. If somebody loved me, I would live.

But that wasn't going to happen. I am sick. A Greek tragedy, not a fairy tale. On the one hand, it was the first time I'd let myself be so unbridled and vulnerable. On the one hand, no one has ever loved me for that.

The hyperloop lover moved away. The building's hot tub continued to be the site of my finding new sexual partners. Dating seemed pointless. I was already having to bring my friends into the fragility of my body in ways I never wanted. I'd be lying naked while my very first love tried to contort my spastic muscle back into a workable shoulder. Or I'd have to let my longtime friend—a mother—wrap her whole body around me when she realized I could no longer regulate my body temperature.

Sex wasn't going to save me. Medicine would. But if sex was the hump I was using to get through the diagnostic hurdles, another tool in my arsenal, I wanted it to feel meaningful, not essential.

I stopped.

•

I've read Audre Lorde's "Uses of the Erotic: The Erotic as Power" at least once every year since my twenties. Eroticism is indigo for me, not a text, I barely remember the words. But what I try to remember most when I'm hurting is that the closer we are to the erotic, the more devalued we are by all forms of masculine power. Because I am sexy, I am suspect. And because I believe this is powerful, I am alone.

Lorde says "love in all its forms" is "born of chaos." Eros, the erotic, is the assertion of our life force. I have never felt closer to the source of creation than when I've been ill. I have felt defeated by life, cheated by it, but learned to submit to it with compassion. That sense is orgasmic—a tensing and weakening of the flesh.

Everyone living is dying. And because I am dying, I desire pleasure as proof that I have lived. The nearness of death to sex drives us to feel love. But we are caught in a system that attempts to replace love, the harmonic chaos of raw human emotion, with regulation and prescriptive certainty. It's reduced sex to sensation—something to get, something to get past, something to have to make you feel sexy—when sex is an alignment of our spiritual and political selves.

And so is illness. Both sickness and sex demand that we look at our bodies as the site of spiritual and political warfare. COVID-19 and the AIDS epidemic. Paternity leave and *Roe v. Wade*. It doesn't matter what we want (or who we want). From birth, our health is the pursuit of two questions: "What will cause us to die?" and "Who determines how we live?"

In between those two questions is our lives, us pretending to be free. Disease. Famine. Religion. Government. The life we normalize is a mirage. A belief that we move freely—unmediated, unregulated—and we choose a healthy lifestyle and, therefore, are rewarded for it when other people suffer. In the droll certainty that we are "free," disability and erotic desire are hard to look at. We don't want to be reminded how little we are in control. We don't want to believe it. We don't want to see ourselves. How honest we are. How painful and utterly, unbelievably sensual.

It's my disabled friends, my chronically ill friends, who have been the best lovers to themselves. This surprised me. Because when I was living on the other side of healthy I didn't realize there was more to ask for of sex than the mundane; the sensation was powerful enough. It wasn't until the pandemic that I even started to question a potential beyond that, when quarantine made "normal" relationships out of the question. Specifically, I was talking to a longtime friend of mine, a poet, who had suffered from a series of "invisible" disabilities for years. For years she had chosen to be celibate. But not without a clear relationship to her own erotic enjoyment. She told me, "I've learned to enjoy a really healthy sex life with myself."

I pondered it. I'd grown up with the prejudice that touching yourself was frowned upon. Even after I'd broken all conventional edicts of whom I might partner with and how, the idea that I might enjoy myself seemed oddly selfish. I already enjoyed living by myself, spending time with myself. Partnering with someone even briefly seemed like admitting to needing the people I had left.

I bought my first sex toy, the Rabbit, after my divorce.

Thinking of sex this way felt new. The autonomy was efficient, pleasurable, but not much fun. I wasn't looking for sex that was erotic. I wasn't looking for sex that was erotic. I was looking for sex without the imagined requirement of intimacy. The latter was hard to find in people, the former was all that a sexy toy could provide. I wasn't looking for porn or pictures. I missed that union. That connection to another soul. I don't mean those thoughts romantically. I mean them biologically. It's science. I couldn't trigger enough oxytocin to make sex with myself useful. I wasn't thinking of myself as an equal partner in my own delight.

I'm surprised how comfortable we've grown with twenty-first-century kink, but not with sex toys. Kink is radio friendly; talk around toys is pretty hush quiet. I believe it's the same conundrum I experienced. It's a clear, chemical turn-on to talk about what you want to do to someone or have someone do to you. But to be able to carry on a conversation about how you charm yourself, enchant yourself, utterly thrill yourself, feels kinda strange. But living outside of normalcy is essential to our survival on a sick planet, a dying world. And more than that, knowing how to turn yourself on is undeniably healthy.

And erotic. Healing is pleasure. When the process is hard, the pleasure is more intense. That doesn't mean easy to achieve, it means hard-earned. And there's nothing more erotic than release. Getting healed for me has been about truly letting go, whether that meant recovering from convention or from a chronic illness.

I remember the first time I locked eyes with someone after my divorce was finalized. It was in an elevator. The silence was immaculate. We never talked or touched but as we exited, my insides stirred like a bird cage. I let go of control. I was free.

I met Nefertiti at the end of a reading of the *Sex and the Single Woman* anthology at the Salt Eaters Bookshop in Inglewood. I was three months away from a fourth surgery. I was wearing a neck brace. It'd been nearly a year since my diagnosis, and I'd run out of steam in believing I could be someone to somebody in the state of my illness, including myself. I was defeated. The book talk revived me. The Q and A turned into a full-on conversation about our sex lives. In response to a question, I told a young reader that I'd love to see us normalize more intimacy in our daily lives. After the reading, Nefertiti came up and held my hand.

She owned a concierge pleasure shop down the block from the bookshop. It was called Ghettoff, like the Prince song. Kismet. We talked about our shared heritage of religious upbringing and first marriages. And sickness. She and her longtime partner were both breast cancer survivors. They owned the shop together. For both of us, sickness had redefined the ways we looked at pleasure, but Nefertiti was open about the way illness had reshaped her sense of the erotic in a way I was still hesitant to. What used to work for me had changed. And the kind of sexy object I had felt like at the beginning of my diagnosis had dissipated. More and more, I felt like being around people less and less.

"Maybe I'll just be a ho," I'd declared to a chronically ill friend soon after sex became the prescription for my diagnosis. She frowned at me. She encouraged me to think of other ways to approach orgasming, like a relationship. But the worse I got, the less I wanted anyone in my world. To act like I felt better than I did grew harder and harder, even temporarily. And even my friend, as a chronically ill married person, confessed how difficult it was to feel like an adequate partner in the ebb and flow of treatments and relapses. It would be easier if "sex" were a once-saved-always-saved remedy. But the healing I got from feeling sensual was wrestling more and more with my desire for privacy. There was only one thing I could do.

Ghettoff is appointment only. Nefertiti and her team of consultants treat each of their clients privately, carefully, like a patient. She poured me a glass of sweet brown liquor—medicine—and we talked. We talked about what I want to feel. I'd never had this conversation divorced from someone I wanted to have sex with. Wait . . . the person I was trying to turn on in this situation was me. There I was, beside myself, with myself, having a glass of cognac, describing what made me happy. I described the feelings I got from different forms of stimulation and Nefertiti introduced me to assistants who could supply that support, and beyond: prosthetics. My needs are increasingly cyclical.

The sweetest story Nefertiti told me was about the night, early in their relationship, that she and her partner unveiled their sex toys. The conversation of kink and bright colors (vibrators, dildos, restraints, plugs) reminded me of my synesthesia. In remission, Nefertiti was still healing from the last of her breast reconstruction procedures. I was still in a cervical brace. We were talking about sex. I couldn't believe it.

I don't know where I inherited the concept of shame in my body around both disability and sex, but I know it's deepseated. I can definitely say few people have given me as much license to be human as Nefertiti, allowing me the freedom to be both a sexual being and a sick one. A sick person who is also a sexual being—I didn't talk about the need for the erotic as some kind of prescription for my frailty, I talked about being sensual as something I needed simply because it makes me feel good.

Once I felt comfortable, we moved away from the sex I wanted in the moment, and on to what I might want in the future. In the future, how would I want a partner to make me feel, or me them? This was a question I'd only let myself answer in the moments when sex seemed imminent, not a continual proposition. I loved it. Fantasizing about what a prosthetic might help my sick body do sexually. I was using them to walk, to live, to hold my head in the correct place— why couldn't I also think of them as an enhancement of other powers? I felt pleasure, like Kali, all over again.

Sex in all its forms is something we all can attend to. However it pleases us. You don't have to feel young, or healthy, or perfect. There is art in the delight of healing, and therefore beauty. Like wabi-sabi, the Japanese art concept that there is beauty in the unbalanced and in aged things because they speak to the impermanence of time. Or kintsugi, the practice within wabi-sabi, in which that impermanence is fortified with seams of gold. How we tend to ourselves in the time that we have is precious. How we hold ourselves is valuable. Medicine work.

And sometimes, when I truly let go, I see gold shining through the cracks of a love I thought I could only have for another. We are the gold. We believe we are the gold shining through the cracks of what we love, when we are the gold itself. Molten warmth and cool currency. Not just ornament but element. Our pleasure is essential to living. And as long as I am living, I choose life.

On Liberation

St. George's, Bermuda

It wasn't freedom I was looking for, it was liberation. I never wanted to go it alone. Freedom is no good as a single body. But sometimes I was all I had. Because I was looking to liberate, and not save. For the latter, I had all the imagination in the world but not the strength required. When people have abandoned me, I have realized this is sometimes why. Because I was free. And I offered my freedom up freely. Audacious, invasive, arrogant—I presented a portal but offered no salvation. Not because I didn't want to, but because I was too frail to.

My body kept failing me but not my spirit. How paradoxical. I've been traveling the world looking for salvation, only to find the only salvation we are each guaranteed is the one we give birth to in our own bodies. How we present or choose to believe is irrelevant. It's about how far we've come in removing our sense of responsibility to death.

Nearly every day in Bermuda I stand at the edge of the water and say not today. By both surviving and not living in shame at the fact that I've survived, wholly imperfect and ignorant, I have not made Death my champion for at least one more moment. I've done better than survived; I have lived.

It's not a surprise to me that Shakespeare's *The Tempest* was written about here. I've never read the work, although I loved to quote Shakespeare at four a.m. in bars back when four a.m. in bars was still a thing for me. But the word is how I'm filled. A violent windy storm of unrest. I write intentionally. I work hard knowing that the work will not be finished. I dream of a world in which I am dead and I've left behind at least a page that is a map out of this goddamn torrent.

It wasn't freedom I ever wanted, not at all—it was you, I wanted you.

At the beach, a gray-headed man from Massachusetts keeps gazing around the specter of my shadow trying to read my furious cursive. (Intrusive in a way he's allowed to be, that descendant of ships that marked our destiny . . .)

"What are you writing?" he demands of me while I sit on a rock, in a bikini, tending to the business I hope will someday be yours.

I'm writing. Obviously. I have a story to tell, part myth and part autobiography. It seems strange to him that I would sit down in the midst of the ocean—Black, femme, abused, some-times paralyzed, lover of self and all forms of expression—and record the fact I did this. He needs to know my occupation. The fact that I am occupied in my current task isn't meaning-ful enough. I am a writer, I tell him, and a college professor. "You can't be!" he says. "You look so young!" His reaction is typical. I don't look too young to be what I am, I just look like someone whom the world would make make their money dif-ferently. Whom a different path would have afforded time alone on an island. It's why liberation sticks with me—the need to break tradition, I mean really destroy it, until nothing of this logic is ever logical again. But it's tricky. Unloosening the misconceptions of professorship he's already formed, he quizzes me on scholars who taught where I did but have long since retired. Why. I refuse to pass and so he leaves not believ-ing me. He googles me hours later and messages me on Insta-gram in the torrent of his discovery: "You're real! I can't believe it!"

I dropped out of the conversation loop as quickly as possible. I was back home in Brooklyn by then, and had little time to question if I was real or not as I shuffled back and forth be-tween neurologists and orthopedic surgeons. I hoped my body would hit some kind of stasis. That never came. But, one day, another direct message did. It was the man from Massachusetts introducing me to Kristin, a local Bermudian bookseller. "I met another Black woman here and she is just like you!" I was skeptical given his penchant for exclamation points. But when he was right, she and I chalked it up to the reality that anyone can be a messenger for our ancestors if they're standing directly in the line of reception. When I returned to Bermuda the following month—my legs still collapsing, and the waters still, warm—we cheered to his good fortune over rum.

"He came into my bookstore hollering about how he had just met an American writer just like me, AND he didn't buy nothin'!" was the truncated tale of her brief encounter with our connector. But that's the trouble with how little I can offer of liberation on the page. You deserve to be there, surrounded by the White Horse Pub's scent of beer-stained hardwood and decent cologne. The oldest bar in the oldest port settlement on the island. The settlement, a World Heritage Site, a tiny stretch of historical island. Land in the transatlantic where the original Black settlers were free.

Freedom is funny and fleeting. No matter where I've traveled it has been inevitable that a country's account of the freedom of its people contains some comparison to, or record of, my own. Although the first black people who came to Bermuda were free, slavery also began in Bermuda a few years earlier than the first ships had arrived in Jamestown—with black

people from Africa, Latin Americans, and American Indians—
and ended officially in the British colony roughly thirty years
earlier than it did on the independent coastline. Freedom
is tricky. When it comes to the displaced and darker skinned,
the date when freedom is bestowed—if we can say such a
thing—is a history held by most of the world. But the language always troubles me.

How and when was freedom earned by the people who
write down that they offered it?

That night, making my way from the pub back to the place
where I'm staying, I pop into a cigar shop named after Winston Churchill. I purchase a Cuban. I sit on the property of
my Airbnb trying to teach myself to blow smoke rings into
the moonlight. One of the apartment tenants, Jamaican, an
engineer at the new airport Bermuda is building, stops by to
say hello. "You're so free . . . ," he offers at the close of our conversation instead of good night. It's the first time anyone has
said that to me and meant it nicely.

Freedom is the state of being nothing. Not nothing, but
zero. The state of being null, an indivisible integer. Because
you have been broken, you are invisible. Because you know
who you are when you're broken, you have achieved the divine. Those who are disabled, those who are queer, those
miscalculated, or misguided. Those who are any one of you.
Whomever you are when the world says you shouldn't be. I
carry you—0—my incandescent bubble. My whole universe.

We are a strange and beautiful people. Because of that, we will survive. It is why I love the water. I remember you. Each of us bubbling up under, eroding the shoreline, they remember you too. This is the freedom that scares people. The one that reveals how insecure our borders are—because they are only weaknesses. If we have to fight until there is no one left, love will survive because it has to.

I thought a lot about abolition during the pandemic. While we all crunched ourselves into some man's pockets, like mass death was business as usual, and the rich took trips around the Earth in spaceships. We were frightened. We drowned in the anxiousness of our gasps under masks and doused our vegetables in chemicals in the bathtub. Local hospitals erected circus tents to hold all the bodies, mass graves. And, of course, this meant that those who claimed freedom, but who, honestly, must have never felt it, started to take Black people out—one by one—and the world noticed because, in its solitude, there was so little else to see.

We are matter, we said. Some of it was fake. Much of it didn't last. But it at least shifted long enough for the people-who-saw-themselves-as-free to understand what they thought they had to give and take—how they perceived it—was entirely fictional. Their "freedom," just like everyone else's, was doled out for us by whom we worked for and what we consumed—on the cheap and at irregular intervals. The "freedom to . . . ," "the freedom of . . . ," and "the freedom for . . ." You can't just give freedom, and we certainly aren't born with it because we pledge allegiance to a flag. Freedom is our consciousness, when we keep it. So freedom is not what we were looking for, not at all.

•

I'm struggling to find an adequate grocery store to do my shopping. The strange thing about living on an island like Bermuda is knowing the soil is fertile but your resources are scarce. I am banned from that abundance by the supermarkets and restaurants, where most of the food is expensive, imported, and curated to colonial taste. The sterile shelves in the small market at the center of St. George's were dedicated to the wasteful continental palate: the "freedom to" eat exactly the way the British would have, had they never left home. Yes, strange. Since so much of their expansion was cargo ships full of spices, sugar, tobacco to expand their palate, you would think . . . but a few hundred years later, every country with the queen on their currency keeps their shelves stocked with nothing but mayo.

I wanted bananas. I went into the store only to lift and put down the oversize Chiquita monstrosities that had been shipped in from a plantation my former husband and I once accidentally passed hiking in Nicaragua. The workers, dark and angular—their look almost unchanged from that of their ancestors who became some of Bermuda's first enslaved settlers, their backs still chained and heavy, carrying stalks of bananas the size of palace chandeliers. The overseers on the perimeter leaned against machetes, assault rifles thrown lazily over their shoulders as they chatted like a military junta. It was unclear if the weaponry was intended to keep us outsiders, or the workers, from eating. But it was clear in their eyes the unofficial answer was both.

"Well, that's not how I thought we got bananas," we said to each other as we stopped holding our breath. We slipped back into the proper hiking trails of the jungle. We had spent so much time eating bananas in the "freedom from" other people's suffering. For years after, "jungle" was a dirty word to me—as "black" is to those who have not accepted our freedom as possible. I was ashamed of what I saw. I couldn't eat them because of what I knew, and I couldn't go to an unknown supermarket without seeing a bunch with the appealing blue sticker of the woman smiling—the fruit upon her head plentiful. There she was again in Bermuda. The banana woman—stiff, light green, and familiar. For a week I would pass them every day in the store, picking up iced tea and bags of crisps on my way to the beach. I watched them struggle to ripen in the store racks, their elongated stems bruising weak and ugly, until they were thrown out and replaced by the next batch sent by the junta. The cycle continued. I still couldn't eat them, but my hunger grew.

And then in Bermuda, I began eating bananas again. On my walk to the beach I passed groves of sweet jade gems behind the house once owned by a set of well-to-do sisters. Banana Manor, Kristin said the name was, the sisters taunting me. After coveting them often, I pointed them out as Kristin took me through a historical tour of the center of town. We plotted. She started in on a roguish attempt to figure out how we might liberate them, their tiny perfection ripening to tobacco, then rotting. There was a stone wall that once separated these two rich white women from the sizable homes of free blacks that surrounded them. Kristin stood on a stone in a flowing blue skirt, peering over the walled garden, concocting a plan of acquisition. The sun was too bright in the day, and the bananas too far inland from the fence, to trespass with a foreigner. But she hadn't given up hope. She marked in her memory to ask an older, revolutionary friend of hers.

"I'll ask Suzanne," Kristin said. "She'll know." Suzanne was a white Bermudian who had participated in the revolutionary uprisings of Black people in more than a passing way. Suzanne's participation was a prerequisite to her becoming one of Kristin's closest friends. I admired this. I had not in my own freedom been able to hold the white people I cared about to the task of aiding and abetting. But it made a difference. It was January 2021. I wanted no more pictures of white liberals I knew wearing Black Lives Matter masks and carrying Black Lives Matter signs in my social feeds. I wanted to be surrounded by people whose color I didn't have to think about. Not because it didn't matter, but because we'd moved beyond a feeling that that was the fight—to matter—when in reality we are all fighting for the right to live well. I don't believe that's impossible. I only believe we've been duped into thinking freedom is more important than liberty.

I am an idealist. I believe in liberated bananas and revolutionary friends who know how to get them.

I want to believe I am part of a world where friends inspire each other to set each other free. Not euphemistically, I want to believe in the world.

As for the bananas, I never made it to the other side of the fence, but I was handed a bevvy of browning yellow beauties by a healer I visited—growing fresh in his garden. He saw how long my eyes lingered on them and offered them willingly. There was no need for me to scheme and pilfer. "You look like these will do you good," he said. The land provided the man who provided. Liberation is like that.

If you know where to look, life in Bermuda is being liberated everywhere. Sometimes when Kristin and Suzanne took long walks home, they would pluck sprigs of rosemary and thyme from the garden of a bed-and-breakfast that had been owned by another revolutionary friend. The friend had to let the hotel succumb to the pandemic, and as a last gift to her neighbors, she let the gardens go to seed instead of cutting them down. The herbs grew wild everywhere, blossoms littered with fragrant leaves. Geckos and beetles burrowed into the brick, leaving a bounty for the local cats. The cats would catch and eat them, and frighten away more pestilent vermin. And short, fat trees built canopies for birds, hovels for the twitching noses of rabbits. Nothing was in order but everyone was fed; you could hear singing.

"Freedom" is a word that expects an emptiness in the loss of ownership. Liberation takes pride in what it can't foresee, and finds pride in what it can return to. I lose the comfort of blue stickers at the supermarket, but the bananas in my life are homegrown and abundant, born of a life that is wild and free. That is freedom because of liberation, the best of both kinds.

●

Wild and free. There is a shame I carry with me for being called both; I was taught to hide any sense of myself in a deep shroud of modesty. It's my American heritage. *We hold these truths to be* contradictory. Some of us cling to a Declaration of Independence, the rest of us cling to autobiography. Writing ourselves before history does it for us.

Mary Prince was that kind of person, Kristin tells me proudly as we're standing in the sun, surrounded by St. George's oldest historical buildings, the old courthouse and the first port. Mary Prince was the first woman to publish her autobiography in England: *The History of Mary Prince, a West Indian*

Slave. The book went through three printings in its first year, 1831. Prince's book exposed the brutality of slavery so clearly that her words dismantled slavery throughout the British Empire. Great Britain's Slavery Abolition Act was passed by Parliament two years after the publication of her book. Although the first line in Mary Prince's memoir is its preface—a man's word, not hers—it's an important statement: "The idea of writing Mary Prince's history was first suggested by herself."

Autobiography has never been an easy calling. In Fred Moten's *In the Break*, the philosopher mentions the importance of people like Mary Prince double- and triple-authenticating their memoirs in their titles, subtitles, and early pages because of the number of discreditors around them. No one wanted to believe a person completely broken, physically and mentally, would be able to respond back, in love. To say "I exist" because it will save the whole world. We were selling millions of people across waters as livestock. Our humanity would never survive that. Mary Prince saw that and wrote down her story. She liberated the world.

But authenticity isn't easy. Prince testified in two lawsuits for libel filed against her book's publisher in 1833 that rebuked Mary's accounts of slavery as inaccurate and defamatory. What had Mary said? "The man that says slaves be quite happy in slavery—that they don't want to be free—that man is either ignorant or a lying person. I never heard a slave say so."

It took me nine years to find a publisher who would take my writing a travel memoir seriously. The most serious criticism I received claimed that being who I am and seeing the world as I have is an unrelatable narrative. As if you aren't out here, as if the reason I write doesn't exist. That's why freedom is too hard a fight. It relies on one unreliable narrative. That we were slaves. That a person can be property to begin with. Memoir is liberation by independence. It is our abolitionist movement.

"Who told you you deserved meat?" Kristin says on our tour, with Shakespearean gravitas. It is a line of cross-examination Kristin discovered examining Prince's court documents for an essay she is writing. The question stuck out to me because of how often, and in how many ways, I've been asked it. As if I, like everyone else, don't have the right to be.

"I did," Mary Prince answered. "I told myself I should have meat." And somehow, two hundred years since, *I'm consumed by how often I let someone else dictate how I feel and what I take in*. It is not just the world that punishes the "wild and free"— who really are, at their core, just honest. It is me. *I* forget what I should have. I forget to let me have what I need. Who is free? Not me. Not that person. I need liberation. I offer it to everyone. But, just like you, I am far too vulnerable to leave my liberation up to anyone else.

•

On my last day in Bermuda we went foraging. The sky drizzles a clean mist over the vegetation so that what we harvested is covered in globes—glass beads of dew we shook from the leaves.

We listen to the folds of the ocean. The ocean tides pummeled the beach at night, and when the tides retreat and the sand dries, the remaining leaves scatter across the shore in a keen sheen of salt. And in the crags where small crustaceans take shelter, still-damp herbs leave the air thick in coriander and aloe.

And Yesha is standing beside me. Yesha, the writer for whom, like me, traveling to make a life she loved was just a beginning. She is standing beside me in her origin story—looking at the land that made her anew. She's a Bermuda college professor now instead of an aspiring Minnesota pop star. She liberates one lush piece of spinach growing from a stalk amid the rock and can't believe her mouth. These greens, which grow as wild and free as any music verse that ever moved her, fill her like a sonnet. "So perfectly seasoned," Yesha says, snapping her fingers and pursing her lips; she was almost moved to poetry.

Liberation is a beginning.

It's finding a new home in your old one. It had been over ten years since Yesha's first trip to Minneapolis. She had canvassed the world since, looking for freedom, to finally find it foraging in Bermuda. To find in her hometown a "welcome" just as fresh for her as it was for me. This was the freedom we'd been looking for, the liberation we needed. A homecoming.

"Jesus, mon, that's wicked!" Yesha said to her girlfriend Corynne. She hopped around and snapped her fingers like the tips were covered in a hot verse. "And it just comes up out the ground like this?! You mean this has just been sitting here growing this whole time?!" Kristin, Suzanne, and our tour guide Doreen just laughed. Sara tugged my arm. We had just met but somewhere in the mist had made a secret pact that we'd care for each other forever. She'd spotted three light blue eggs nestled in a ground nest. Doreen picked it up and told us a story I've long since forgotten.

Doreen could trace her family roots all the way back to the early ships where her family—doctors and scientists on the other coast—took up the same tradition of seeking, finding liberation, on what was meant to be their captive island. Starting with the flat plantain leaves that grew gnarled and plentiful under our feet, a cure for scurvy. I imagine the leaves greeting them as a sign: despite the perils of the journey, we would survive. We chewed purple-flowered succulents that prevented cavities, and sucked the stems of nasturtiums, like fiery honeysuckle, before consuming the petals. Good for the sinuses. Good to the soul.

At the end of our foraging journey we sat in the mist and

shared vegan cookies and squash soup seasoned entirely with herbs she'd introduced us to on our outing. Kristin, our organizer, was so ecstatic about the goods, she had already made plans to pack what was left of the take to bring with us for our feast that evening. We were full and would continue to be full. We were filled and the festival of that filling would continue. The sweet biscuits tickled our feet and the stew warmed the soft pockets of our mouths. There were flowers in the break of each bite, nasturtiums and crumbled hibiscus. The blossoms were so plentiful on my regular walk, I marveled for the first time at how often I missed that my world was lush to be eaten.

Love is here. Love has been sitting here this whole time. Some days in this world are easy. Some days, liberation just finds you. Sometimes it's a day or a month or more, but I pray, for you, a lifetime. May you have a life of beauty. One that tastes good. One where you are stunned by its smallest revelations.

Who told you you should be free? I did. Freedom is traveling but liberation is food. No matter where you are, may you always be certain who you are. And when you are, get everything you deserve.

The laptop clasps as the plane descends
(wherever you go, pound these grounds into myth).

Acknowledgments

This book only exists because of an overwhelming and re-plenishing well of love and support. It wouldn't be possible to name everyone, so I hope that you read this and know my heart includes you in this collective thank-you. Thank you for your kindness. Thank you for your patient tending. Thank you for not abandoning me in my lows or giving up on me in my frailty. Humanity is a fragile ecosystem. I'm so grateful we have each other.

About the Author

Shayla Lawson lives.